WITHDRAWN

At Issue

| WikiLeaks

Other Books in the At Issue Series:

At Issue

|WikiLeaks

Tamara Thompson, Book Editor

GREENHAVEN PRESS
A part of Gale, Cengage Learning

GALE
CENGAGE Learning·

Detroit • New York • San Francisco • New Haven, Conn • Waterville, Maine • London

Elizabeth Des Chenes, *Director, Publishing Solutions*

© 2013 Greenhaven Press, a part of Gale, Cengage Learning.

Gale and Greenhaven Press are registered trademarks used herein under license.

For more information, contact:
Greenhaven Press
27500 Drake Rd.
Farmington Hills, MI 48331-3535
Or you can visit our Internet site at gale.cengage.com

Articles in Greenhaven Press anthologies are often edited for length to meet page requirements. In addition, original titles of these works are changed to clearly present the main thesis and to explicitly indicate the author's opinion. Every effort is made to ensure that Greenhaven Press accurately reflects the original intent of the authors. Every effort has been made to trace the owners of copyrighted material.

Cover photograph reproduced with permission of Brand X Pictures.

LIBRARY OF CONGRESS CATALOGING-IN-PUBLICATION DATA

WikiLeaks / Tamara Thompson, book editor.
    p. cm. -- (At issue)
    Includes bibliographical references and index.
    ISBN 978-0-7377-6219-8 (hardcover) -- ISBN 978-0-7377-6220-4 (pbk.)
    1. WikiLeaks (Organization) 2. Leaks (Disclosure of information)--Political aspects. I. Thompson, Tamara.
    JF1525.W45W547 2012
    025.06'3--dc23

                                                                2012008969

Printed in the United States of America
1 2 3 4 5 6 7 16 15 14 13 12

Contents

Introduction

Even though it had been publishing private, secret, and classified information from anonymous government sources and corporate whistleblowers worldwide since 2006, few Americans had ever heard of the organization called WikiLeaks until April 2010, when it uploaded a classified video to its website showing a US military helicopter gunning down civilians and journalists in Baghdad, the capital of Iraq. Overnight, WikiLeaks was transformed from an obscure high-tech curiosity into a major player in the unfolding drama over free speech, democracy, and national security in the age of the Internet.

But the so-called "Collateral Murder" video was only the beginning. Over the next eighteen months, WikiLeaks—a self-identified nonprofit electronic media outlet whose professed mission is to reveal secrets and thereby promote accountable and transparent governments—published nearly seventy-seven thousand classified intelligence documents related to the War in Afghanistan, some four hundred thousand related to the Iraq War (known collectively as the War Logs), and a quarter of a million secret diplomatic cables from the US State Department (known as "Cablegate").

Eventually traced to a US Army private named Bradley Manning who was stationed in Iraq, the leaks constituted the largest security breach in US history, and the unprecedented volume and scope of the classified documents made public by WikiLeaks blindsided the American government. Officials called the disclosures a threat to national security, predicted irreparable harm to US diplomatic relations, and publicly feared that the leaks would endanger the safety of people named in the documents.

High-ranking officials called for disabling WikiLeaks and aggressively prosecuting its founder, Julian Assange. Their various suggestions included assassinating him outright, designating WikiLeaks a terrorist organization and Assange an enemy combatant so he could be held at the Guantanamo Bay military prison in Cuba, and prosecuting Assange under the Espionage Act of 1917. (Assange cannot be charged with treason because he is not an American citizen; he is Australian.)

But for all the strong words and legal posturing, it is not at all clear that WikiLeaks or Assange have broken any American laws. While Manning—who is in military custody facing court martial on twenty-two charges that could imprison him for life—may indeed have acted illegally by downloading and sharing classified information, the legal right of a third party to accept and publish such information—online or in print—is much more complicated.

When the *New York Times* made public the classified Vietnam War documents known as the Pentagon Papers in 1971, the US government brought charges against the *Times*, but the court ruled that the press has a First Amendment right to publish information that is "significant to the people's understanding of their government's policy." The court also said that the *Times* was protected because it did not, itself, illegally acquire the classified information or conspire to do so; it was simply the messenger.

Building on free-speech case law, the US Supreme Court specifically extended First Amendment protection to Internet content in 1997, when it wrote in its decision for *Reno vs. ACLU (American Civil Liberties Union)*: "As a matter of constitutional tradition, in the absence of evidence to the contrary, we presume that governmental regulation of the content of speech is more likely to interfere with the free exchange of ideas than to encourage it. The interest in encouraging freedom of expression in a democratic society outweighs any theoretical but unproven benefit of censorship."

The critical question at issue here is: will WikiLeaks be the case to provide such "evidence to the contrary?" If so, commentators say the precedent set in a decision against WikiLeaks would not only severely curtail free speech on the Internet, it would also imperil the ability of traditional print media outlets to publish information made available to them through sources and leaks and could bring about a de facto end to effective investigative reporting.

As the case continues to unfold and the United States tries to figure out how to best go after Assange and stop WikiLeaks from publishing sensitive information, other circumstances are converging to muffle the now-infamous whistleblower website. In December 2010 alone:

- Like an economic embargo imposed against a hostile nation, online money exchange site PayPal—WikiLeaks's primary funnel for donations—froze the organization's account, saying that its service "cannot be used for any activities that encourage, promote, facilitate, or instruct others to engage in illegal activity." Visa and MasterCard similarly locked WikiLeaks out, and the banking blockade was still in force in early 2012.

- Following a telephone call from US Senator Joe Lieberman, chair of the Senate's Committee on Homeland Security and Governmental Affairs, Internet giant Amazon terminated WikiLeaks's access to its cloud hosting service, which hosted the organization's website and all its data. WikiLeaks was forced to move its site back to European-based servers, where it endures increasingly frequent denial-of-service attacks.

- Assange was arrested in Europe on sexual misconduct charges that are unrelated to WikiLeaks. He maintains his innocence and claims the case against him is politically motivated. As of March 2012, he was still under house arrest in London, England, while fighting extradition to Sweden to face trial.

But even with Assange in legal limbo and fundraising at a trickle, WikiLeaks has managed to publish new leaks, such as nearly eight hundred classified dossiers of Guantanamo Bay prisoners and the December 2011 release of "The Spy Files," hundreds of documents from global intelligence contractors in the incredibly lucrative and secretive mass surveillance industry.

Whether the mountains of information made public by WikiLeaks prove to be "significant to the people's understanding of their government's policy" still remains to be seen, and only the eventual context of history will show which version of the WikiLeaks story will emerge as the mainstream narrative. But one thing is abundantly clear, the views could not represent a starker contrast:

WikiLeaks is a champion of free speech and open government, whose activities deserve legal protection and journalistic accolades; WikiLeaks is a terrorist organization that is aiding the enemy, endangering national security, and jeopardizing the safety of countless individuals.

Julian Assange is a visionary media pioneer whose efforts further truth and democracy; Julian Assange is an enemy of the United States whose main motivation is fame for himself at any expense.

Bradley Manning is a traitor to his country and should be convicted of treason for stealing and leaking classified documents; Bradley Manning is a true American hero for risking his personal freedom to make public the proof of illegal and morally troubling military actions and questionable diplomatic practices.

The authors in *At Issue: WikiLeaks* present a wide range of viewpoints about whether the organization is a friend or foe of free speech and democracy, and they consider what WikiLeaks's actions—and those taken against it—might mean for the future of both print and electronic publishing.

1

WikiLeaks Practices Highly Principled Investigative Journalism

WikiLeaks.org

WikiLeaks is an online media organization that publishes private, secret, and classified information leaked from anonymous news sources and whistleblowers in corporations and government agencies worldwide.

WikiLeaks is a groundbreaking new type of media organization that publishes anonymously leaked classified information and other documents in their entirety online, alongside its own summaries and analyses of the information. By providing all of the raw source material on which its articles are based, WikiLeaks allows its readers to verify for themselves whether its reporting is credible. The organization strongly believes that such transparency is vital to holding governments, corporations, and other institutions accountable for their actions. WikiLeaks believes that publishing information obtained by "principled leaking"—leaks based on moral conscience or the information's importance to society—has the potential to not only expose corruption but to even save lives. WikiLeaks has broken numerous stories in the world press and has been awarded several prestigious journalism awards.

WikiLeaks is a not-for-profit media organisation. Our goal is to bring important news and information to the public. We provide an innovative, secure and anonymous way

Julian Assange, "What Is WikiLeaks?," WikiLeaks.org, September 1, 2011. Reproduced by permission.

for sources to leak information to our journalists (our electronic drop box). One of our most important activities is to publish original source material alongside our news stories so readers and historians alike can see evidence of the truth. We are a young organisation that has grown very quickly, relying on a network of dedicated volunteers around the globe. Since 2007, when the organisation was officially launched, WikiLeaks has worked to report on and publish important information. We also develop and adapt technologies to support these activities.

WikiLeaks has sustained and triumphed against legal and political attacks designed to silence our publishing organisation, our journalists and our anonymous sources. The broader principles on which our work is based are the defence of freedom of speech and media publishing, the improvement of our common historical record and the support of the rights of all people to create new history. We derive these principles from the Universal Declaration of Human Rights. In particular, Article 19 inspires the work of our journalists and other volunteers. It states that everyone has the right to freedom of opinion and expression; this right includes freedom to hold opinions without interference and to seek, receive and impart information and ideas through any media and regardless of frontiers. We agree, and we seek to uphold this and the other Articles of the Declaration.

How WikiLeaks Works

WikiLeaks has combined high-end security technologies with journalism and ethical principles. Like other media outlets conducting investigative journalism, we accept (but do not solicit) anonymous sources of information. Unlike other outlets, we provide a high security anonymous drop box fortified by cutting-edge cryptographic information technologies. This provides maximum protection to our sources. We are fearless in our efforts to get the unvarnished truth out to the public. When information comes in, our journalists analyse the material, verify it and write a news piece about it describing its significance to society. We then publish both the news story and the original material in order to enable readers to analyse the story in the context of the original source material themselves. Our news stories are in the comfortable presentation style of Wikipedia, although the two organisations are not otherwise related. Unlike Wikipedia, random readers can not edit our source documents.

As the media organisation has grown and developed, WikiLeaks been developing and improving a harm minimisation procedure. We do not censor our news, but from time to time we may remove or significantly delay the publication of some identifying details from original documents to protect life and limb of innocent people.

Better scrutiny leads to reduced corruption and stronger democracies in all society's institutions, including government, corporations and other organizations.

We accept leaked material in person and via postal drops as alternative methods, although we recommend the anonymous electronic drop box as the preferred method of submitting any material. We do not ask for material, but we make sure that if material is going to be submitted it is done securely and that the source is well protected. Because we receive so much information, and we have limited resources, it may take time to review a source's submission.

We also have a network of talented lawyers around the globe who are personally committed to the principles that WikiLeaks is based on, and who defend our media organisation.

Why the Media (and Particularly WikiLeaks) Is Important

Publishing improves transparency, and this transparency creates a better society for all people. Better scrutiny leads to reduced corruption and stronger democracies in all society's institutions, including government, corporations and other organisations. A healthy, vibrant and inquisitive journalistic media plays a vital role in achieving these goals. We are part of that media.

Scrutiny requires information. Historically, information has been costly in terms of human life, human rights and economics. As a result of technical advances—particularly the internet and cryptography—the risks of conveying important information can be lowered. In its landmark ruling on the Pentagon Papers, the US Supreme Court ruled that "only a free and unrestrained press can effectively expose deception in government." We agree.

We believe that it is not only the people of one country that keep their own government honest, but also the people of other countries who are watching that government through the media.

In the years leading up to the founding of WikiLeaks, we observed the world's publishing media becoming less independent and far less willing to ask the hard questions of government, corporations and other institutions. We believed this needed to change.

Publishing the original source material behind each of our stories is the way in which we show the public that our story is authentic.

WikiLeaks has provided a new model of journalism. Because we are not motivated by making a profit, we work cooperatively with other publishing and media organisations around the globe, instead of following the traditional model of competing with other media. We don't hoard our information; we make the original documents available with our news stories. Readers can verify the truth of what we have reported themselves. Like a wire service, WikiLeaks reports stories that are often picked up by other media outlets. We encourage this. We believe the world's media should work together as much as possible to bring stories to a broad international readership.

How WikiLeaks Verifies Its News Stories

We assess all news stories and test their veracity. We send a submitted document through a very detailed examination procedure. Is it real? What elements prove it is real? Who would have the motive to fake such a document and why? We use traditional investigative journalism techniques as well as more modern technology-based methods. Typically we will do a forensic analysis of the document, determine the cost of forgery, means, motive, opportunity, the claims of the apparent authoring organisation, and answer a set of other detailed questions about the document. We may also seek external verification of the document. For example, for our release of the Collateral Murder video, we sent a team of journalists to Iraq to interview the victims and observers of the helicopter attack. The team obtained copies of hospital records, death certificates, eye witness statements and other corroborating evidence supporting the truth of the story. Our verification process does not mean we will never make a mistake, but so far our method has meant that WikiLeaks has correctly identified the veracity of every document it has published.

By definition, intelligence agencies want to hoard information. By contrast, WikiLeaks has shown that it wants to do just the opposite.

Publishing the original source material behind each of our stories is the way in which we show the public that our story is authentic. Readers don't have to take our word for it; they can see for themselves. In this way, we also support the work of other journalism organisations, for they can view and use the original documents freely as well. Other journalists may well see an angle or detail in the document that we were not aware of in the first instance. By making the documents freely available, we hope to expand analysis and comment by all the media. Most of all, we want readers to know the truth so they can make up their own minds.

The People Behind WikiLeaks

WikiLeaks is a project of the Sunshine Press. It's probably pretty clear by now that WikiLeaks is not a front for any intelligence agency or government despite a rumour to that effect. This rumour was started early in WikiLeaks' existence, possibly by the intelligence agencies themselves. WikiLeaks is an independent global group of people with a long standing dedication to the idea of a free press and the improved transparency in society that comes from this. The group includes accredited journalists, software programmers, network engineers, mathematicians and others.

To determine the truth of our statements on this, simply look at the evidence. By definition, intelligence agencies want to hoard information. By contrast, WikiLeaks has shown that it wants to do just the opposite. Our track record shows we go to great lengths to bring the truth to the world without fear or favour.

The great American president Thomas Jefferson once observed that the price of freedom is eternal vigilance. We believe the journalistic media plays a key role in this vigilance.

Anonymity for Sources

As far as we can ascertain, WikiLeaks has never revealed any of its sources. We can not provide details about the security of our media organisation or its anonymous drop box for sources because to do so would help those who would like to compromise the security of our organisation and its sources. What we can say is that we operate a number of servers across multiple international jurisdictions and we we do not keep logs. Hence these logs can not be seized. Anonymization occurs early in the WikiLeaks network, long before information passes to our web servers. Without specialized global internet traffic analysis, multiple parts of our organisation must conspire with each other to strip submitters of their anonymity.

However, we also provide instructions on how to submit material to us, via net cafes, wireless hot spots and even the post so that even if WikiLeaks is infiltrated by an external agency, sources can still not be traced. Because sources who are of substantial political or intelligence interest may have their computers bugged or their homes fitted with hidden video cameras, we suggest that if sources are going to send WikiLeaks something very sensitive, they do so away from the home and work.

WikiLeaks has released more classified intelligence documents than the rest of the world press combined.

A number of governments block access to any address with WikiLeaks in the name. There are ways around this. WikiLeaks has many cover domains, . . . that don't have the organisation in the name. It is possible to write to us or ask around for other cover domain addresses. Please make sure the cryptographic certificate says wikileaks.org.

WikiLeaks's Journalism Record

WikiLeaks is the winner of:

- the 2008 Economist Index on Censorship Freedom of Expression award
- the 2009 Amnesty International human rights reporting award (New Media)

WikiLeaks has a history breaking major stories in major media outlets and robustly protecting sources and press freedoms. We have never revealed a source. We do not censor material. Since formation in 2007, WikiLeaks has been victorious over every legal (and illegal) attack, including those from the Pentagon, the Chinese Public Security Bureau, the Former president of Kenya, the Premier of Bermuda, Scientology, the Catholic & Mormon Church, the largest Swiss private bank, and Russian companies. WikiLeaks has released more classified intelligence documents than the rest of the world press combined.

Principled leaking has changed the course of history for the better. It can alter the course of the present, and it can lead us to a better future.

Some of the stories WikiLeaks has broken include:

- War, killings, torture and detention
- Government, trade and corporate transparency
- Suppression of free speech and a free press
- Diplomacy, spying and (counter-)intelligence
- Ecology, climate, nature and sciences
- Corruption, finance, taxes, trading
- Censorship technology and internet filtering
- Cults and other religious organizations
- Abuse, violence, violation . . .

Importance of Principled Leaking to Journalism, Good Government, and a Healthy Society

Principled leaking has changed the course of history for the better. It can alter the course of history in the present, and it can lead us to a better future.

Consider Daniel Ellsberg, working within the US government during the Vietnam War. He comes into contact with the Pentagon Papers, a meticulously kept record of military and strategic planning throughout the war. Those papers reveal the depths to which the US government has sunk in deceiving the American people about the war. Yet the public and the media know nothing of this urgent and shocking information. Indeed, secrecy laws are being used to keep the public ignorant of gross dishonesty practised by their own government. In spite of those secrecy laws and at great personal risk, Ellsberg manages to disseminate the Pentagon papers to journalists and to the world. Despite criminal charges against Ellsberg, eventually dropped, the release of the Pentagon Papers shocks the world, exposes the government lying and helps to shorten the war and save thousands of both American and Vietnamese lives.

The power of principled leaking to call governments, corporations and institutions to account is amply demonstrated through recent history. The public scrutiny of otherwise unaccountable and secretive institutions forces them to consider the ethical implications of their actions. Which official will chance a secret, corrupt transaction when the public is likely to find out? What repressive plan will be carried out when it is revealed to the citizenry, not just of its own country, but the world? When the risks of embarrassment and discovery increase, the tables are turned against conspiracy, corruption, exploitation and oppression. Open government answers injustice rather than causing it. Open government exposes and undoes corruption. Open governance is the most effective method of promoting good governance.

Today, with authoritarian governments in power in much of the world, increasing authoritarian tendencies in democratic governments, and increasing amounts of power vested in unaccountable corporations, the need for openness and transparency is greater than ever. WikiLeaks interest is the revelation of the truth. Unlike the covert activities of state intelligence agencies, as a media publisher WikiLeaks relies upon the power of overt fact to enable and empower citizens to bring feared and corrupt governments and corporations to justice.

With its anonymous drop box, WikiLeaks provides an avenue for every government official, every bureaucrat, and every corporate worker, who becomes privy to damning information that their institution wants to hide but the public needs to know. What conscience cannot contain, and institutional secrecy unjustly conceals, WikiLeaks can broadcast to the world. It is telling that a number of government agencies in different countries (and indeed some entire countries) have tried to ban access to WikiLeaks. This is of course a silly response, akin to the ostrich burying its head in the sand. A far better response would be to behave in more ethical ways.

Authoritarian governments, oppressive institutions and corrupt corporations should be subject to the pressure, not merely of international diplomacy, freedom of information laws or even periodic elections, but of something far stronger—the consciences of the people within them.

Sufficient principled leaking in tandem with fearless reporting will bring down administrations that rely on concealing reality from their own citizens.

Should the Press Really Be Free?

In its landmark ruling on the Pentagon Papers, the US Supreme Court ruled that "only a free and unrestrained press can effectively expose deception in government." We agree.

The ruling stated that "paramount among the responsibilities of a free press is the duty to prevent any part of the government from deceiving the people and sending them off to distant lands to die of foreign fevers and foreign shot and shell."

It is easy to perceive the connection between publication and the complaints people make about publication. But this generates a perception bias, because it overlooks the vastness of the invisible. It overlooks the unintended consequences of failing to publish and it overlooks all those who are emancipated by a climate of free speech. Such a climate is a motivating force for governments and corporations to act justly. If acting in a just manner is easier than acting in an unjust manner, most actions will be just.

Sufficient principled leaking in tandem with fearless reporting will bring down administrations that rely on concealing reality from their own citizens.

It is increasingly obvious that corporate fraud must be effectively addressed. In the US, employees account for most revelations of fraud, followed by industry regulators, media, auditors and, finally, the SEC [Securities and Exchange Commission]. Whistleblowers account for around half of all exposures of fraud.

Just like a country, a corrupt or unethical corporation is a menace to all inside and outside it. Corporations will behave more ethically if the world is watching closely.

Exposing Corporate Corruption

Corporate corruption comes in many forms. The number of employees and turnover of some corporations exceeds the population and GDP [gross domestic product] of some nation states. When comparing countries, after observations of population size and GDP, it is usual to compare the system of government, the major power groupings and the civic freedoms available to their populations. Such comparisons can also be illuminating in the case of corporations. . . .

While having a GDP and population comparable to Belgium, Denmark or New Zealand, many of these multi-national corporations have nothing like their quality of civic freedoms and protections. This is even more striking when the regional civic laws the company operates under are weak (such as in West Papua, many African states or even South Korea); there, the character of these corporate tyrannies is unregulated by their civilizing surroundings.

Through governmental corruption, political influence, or manipulation of the judicial system, abusive corporations are able to gain control over the defining element of government, the sole right to deploy coercive force.

Just like a country, a corrupt or unethical corporation is a menace to all inside and outside it. Corporations will behave more ethically if the world is watching closely. WikiLeaks has exposed unethical plans and behaviour in corporations and this as resulted in recompense or other forms of justice for victims.

Could Oppressive Regimes Face Legal Consequences Because of WikiLeaks?

The laws and immunities that are applied in national and international courts, committees and other legal institutions vary, and we can't comment on them in particular. The probative value of documents posted on WikiLeaks in a court of law is a question for courts to decide.

While a secure chain of custody cannot be established for anonymous leaks, these leaks can lead to successful court cases. In many cases, it is easier for journalists or investigators to confirm the existence of a known document through official channels (such as an FOI [Freedom of Information] law or legal discovery) than it is to find this information when starting from nothing. Having the title, author or relevant page numbers of an important document can accelerate an investigation, even if the content itself has not been confirmed. In this way, even unverified information is an enabling jump-off point for media, civil society or official investigations. Principled leaking has been shown to contribute to bringing justice to victims via the court system.

2

WikiLeaks Is Not Journalism of Any Sort

Susan Milligan

Susan Milligan is a political and foreign affairs writer and a contributor to a biography of the late Senator Edward Kennedy.

The Internet is a powerful technology that allows anyone with a computer the ability to be an investigative reporter, but there is a responsibility that comes with such an endeavor if it is to enhance, rather than undermine, democracy. WikiLeaks does not meet the standards of professional journalism because the organization does not thoughtfully evaluate and select the information it disseminates. Rather, WikiLeaks recklessly shares all the information it is given—whether or not it is truly important, serves the public interest, or could cause damage. WikiLeaks does not operate on the standard of the public's right to know, which is a primary tenet of journalism. The organization is interested in nothing more than gaining power and getting attention for itself by spreading information that embarrasses governments.

The Internet has been a tremendously empowering tool for people who have felt their voices have gone unheard by their government, the media, organized religion, and Wall Street. Armed with a laptop, a cell phone camera, and You-Tube, anyone can play investigative reporter, or spy, or even amateur celebrity photographer. On its face, technology can be hugely democratizing.

Unfortunately, these same tools—combined with an angry and disenfranchised public—have led to a destructive trend. Too many people have lost the ability to distinguish between speaking truth to power and just being an irresponsible jerk.

This is how we have come to endure WikiLeaks—and its founder, former computer hacker Julian Assange—in our lives. The organization has released more than a quarter of a million documents related to U.S. diplomacy and foreign policy online. Advance disclosure was given to major news organizations, providing a clue to what WikiLeaks's priority is: getting attention.

Weighing the Public's Right to Know

Some of the information in the documents is not surprising, and—as Glenn Kessler smartly noted in the *Washington Post*'s account—has been long-rumored in diplomatic circles. Some of it is fascinating, providing a window into how countries and their leaders deal with each other. But much of it also deteriorates into pure gossip and accomplishes nothing except to damage delicate negotiations and relationships. This balance is measured all the time by legitimate news organizations when they obtain previously unpublished documents or information. Does the public have a right to know the information? Does the public interest—and public interest cannot be defined as simple prurience—outweigh the dangers releasing the information could cause?

> WikiLeaks has information, and uses it to advance its own power, irrespective of whether the disclosures enhance democracy or national security.

The Pentagon Papers [a leaked classified report about the Vietnam War that was published by the *New York Times* in 1971] fall into the category of documents Americans had the right to know about; reporting troop movements during wartime does not meet that standard. But Assange and his group appear not to have made any attempt at all at making responsible judgments about what to release. The reports of what U.S. diplomats think of various foreign leaders, for example, do nothing to check the behavior or authority of the State Department; they just put a chill on future conversations and observations which necessarily must be frank and private. While the release of the documents is, on its face, a challenge to powerful governments and leaders, it serves more to enhance the power of Assange and WikiLeaks. Armed with a computer, a confidential source, and a list of major media outlets, Assange and his team can make governments afraid or embarrassed. That's not the mission of journalism; it's high-stakes paparazzi behavior.

Secrecy for Its Own Sake

Secrecy for its own sake is not only destructive to democracy; it's often silly. When I was reporting in Ukraine in the 1990s, a Western businessman told me he could not distribute a memo to staffers as he had done in his home country. Initially, he would print out a single memo and list the names of recipients. Each was supposed to read it, check off his or her name, and then send the memo off to the next person on the list. Unfortunately, few did this. They saw information of any kind as power, and to share information was to share power. Employees would read the memo, then quietly put it in their desk drawers. When the businessman realized hardly anyone knew about the holiday office party—since someone on the list considered this secret information he was unwilling to share—the intra-office communication strategy had to change.

But WikiLeaks does not operate according to the standard of the public's right, or need, to know. It is the complete opposite—and paradoxically, the same—as the behavior of the post-communist era Ukrainian staffers. WikiLeaks has information, and uses it to advance its own power, irrespective of whether the disclosures enhance democracy or national security or even the right of Americans to understand how their government operates.

The news organizations which reported the WikiLeaks information cannot be held to the same standard; once the documents were out there (or scheduled to be released online), it was impossible for media outlets to ignore them. Further, the documents are better discussed in context, as newspapers have done. Armed with perhaps the most powerful weapon—a computer—WikiLeaks ought to accept the responsibility that comes with it.

3

The Media Has an Uncomfortable but Necessary Relationship with WikiLeaks

Bill Keller

Bill Keller is the executive editor of The New York Times. *This viewpoint is adapted from his introduction to* Open Secrets: WikiLeaks, War and American Diplomacy *published by* The New York Times.

The New York Times *played an integral role in the WikiLeaks story because WikiLeaks gave the* Times *advance access to the leaked classified documents it possessed. The "War Logs" included half a million military dispatches from the battlefields of Afghanistan and Iraq. The "Embassy Cables" included a quarter of a million communications between the US State Department and its worldwide outposts. The* Times *pored over the voluminous data and did independent research of its own before publishing in-depth articles based on information in the leaked documents. The newspaper also carefully weighed the value and consequences of publishing both the articles and the actual logs and cables (as WikiLeaks did); it ultimately chose to do so but redacted (blacked out) names and details that could endanger individuals. The* Times *considered WikiLeaks founder Julian Assange a source, not a collaborator, and the paper's relationship with the mercurial man was often volatile. Nevertheless, although Assange had his own manipulative agenda, the govern-*

ment should not prosecute WikiLeaks for publishing secret information or create new laws to punish the release of classified information. A free press ensures a free democracy.

This past June [2010], Alan Rusbridger, the editor of *The Guardian*, phoned me and asked, mysteriously, whether I had any idea how to arrange a secure communication. Not really, I confessed. *The Times* doesn't have encrypted phone lines, or a Cone of Silence. Well then, he said, he would try to speak circumspectly. In a roundabout way, he laid out an unusual proposition: an organization called WikiLeaks, a secretive cadre of antisecrecy vigilantes, had come into possession of a substantial amount of classified United States government communications. WikiLeaks's leader, Julian Assange, an eccentric former computer hacker of Australian birth and no fixed residence, offered *The Guardian* half a million military dispatches from the battlefields of Afghanistan and Iraq. There might be more after that, including an immense bundle of confidential diplomatic cables. *The Guardian* suggested—to increase the impact as well as to share the labor of handling such a trove—that *The New York Times* be invited to share this exclusive bounty. The source agreed. Was I interested?

I was interested.

The adventure that ensued over the next six months combined the cloak-and-dagger intrigue of handling a vast secret archive with the more mundane feat of sorting, searching and understanding a mountain of data. As if that were not complicated enough, the project also entailed a source who was elusive, manipulative and volatile (and ultimately openly hostile to *The Times* and *The Guardian*); an international cast of journalists; company lawyers committed to keeping us within the bounds of the law; and an array of government officials who sometimes seemed as if they couldn't decide whether they wanted to engage us or arrest us. By the end of the year, the story of this wholesale security breach had outgrown the story of the actual contents of the secret documents and generated much breathless speculation that something—journalism, diplomacy, life as we know it—had profoundly changed forever.

Doing Due Diligence

Soon after Rusbridger's call, we sent Eric Schmitt, from our Washington [D.C.] bureau, to London. Schmitt has covered military affairs expertly for years, has read his share of classified military dispatches and has excellent judgment and an unflappable demeanor. His main assignment was to get a sense of the material. Was it genuine? Was it of public interest? He would also report back on the proposed mechanics of our collaboration with *The Guardian* and the German magazine *Der Spiegel*, which Assange invited as a third guest to his secret smorgasbord. Schmitt would also meet the WikiLeaks leader, who was known to a few *Guardian* journalists but not to us.

The [Times] reporters came to think of Assange as smart and well educated, extremely adept technologically but arrogant, thin-skinned, conspiratorial and oddly credulous.

Schmitt's first call back to *The Times* was encouraging. There was no question in his mind that the Afghanistan dispatches were genuine. They were fascinating—a diary of a troubled war from the ground up. And there were intimations of more to come, especially classified cables from the entire constellation of American diplomatic outposts. WikiLeaks was holding those back for now, presumably to see how this venture with the establishment media worked out. Over the next few days, Schmitt huddled in a discreet office at *The Guardian*, sampling the trove of war dispatches and discussing the complexities of this project: how to organize and study such a voluminous cache of information; how to securely transport, store and share it; how journalists from three very different publications would work together without compromising their independence; and how we would all assure an appropriate distance from Julian Assange. We regarded Assange throughout as a source, not as a partner or collaborator, but he was a man who clearly had his own agenda.

WikiLeaks and 'Collateral Murder'

By the time of the meetings in London, WikiLeaks had already acquired a measure of international fame or, depending on your point of view, notoriety. Shortly before I got the call from *The Guardian*, *The New Yorker* published a rich and colorful profile of Assange, by Raffi Khatchadourian, who had embedded with the group. WikiLeaks's biggest coup to that point was the release, last April, of video footage taken from one of two U.S. helicopters involved in firing down on a crowd and a building in Baghdad [capital of Iraq] in 2007, killing at least 18 people. While some of the people in the video were armed, others gave no indication of menace; two were in fact journalists for the news agency Reuters. The video, with its soundtrack of callous banter, was horrifying to watch and was an embarrassment to the U.S. military. But in its zeal to make the video a work of antiwar propaganda, WikiLeaks also released a version that didn't call attention to an Iraqi who was toting a rocket-propelled grenade and packaged the manipulated version under the tendentious rubric "Collateral Murder."

_____

Assange was openly contemptuous of the American government and certain that he was a hunted man.

_____

Throughout our dealings, Assange was coy about where he obtained his secret cache. But the suspected source of the video, as well as the military dispatches and the diplomatic cables to come, was a disillusioned U.S. Army private first class named Bradley Manning, who had been arrested and was being kept in solitary confinement. . . .

Assange the Enigma

The reporters came to think of Assange as smart and well educated, extremely adept technologically but arrogant, thin-skinned, conspiratorial and oddly credulous. At lunch one day in *The Guardian*'s cafeteria, Assange recounted with an air of great conviction a story about the archive in Germany that contains the files of the former Communist secret police, the Stasi. This office, Assange asserted, was thoroughly infiltrated by former Stasi agents who were quietly destroying the documents they were entrusted with protecting. The *Der Spiegel* reporter in the group, John Goetz, who has reported extensively on the Stasi, listened in amazement. That's utter nonsense, he said. Some former Stasi personnel were hired as security guards in the office, but the records were well protected.

The embargo was the only condition WikiLeaks would try to impose on us; what we wrote about the material was entirely up to us.

Assange was openly contemptuous of the American government and certain that he was a hunted man. He told the reporters that he had prepared a kind of doomsday option. He had, he said, distributed highly encrypted copies of his entire secret archive to a multitude of supporters, and if WikiLeaks was shut down, or if he was arrested, he would disseminate the key to make the information public. . . .

Embargo Agreements

Assange provided us the data on the condition that we not write about it before specific dates that WikiLeaks planned on posting the documents on a publicly accessible Web site. The Afghanistan documents would go first, after we had a few weeks to search the material and write our articles. The larger cache of Iraq-related documents would go later. Such embargoes—agreements not to publish information before a set date—are commonplace in journalism. Everything from studies in medical journals to the annual United States budget is released with embargoes. They are a constraint with benefits, the principal one being the chance to actually read and reflect on the material before publishing it into public view. As Assange surely knew, embargoes also tend to build suspense and amplify a story, especially when multiple news outlets broadcast it at once. The embargo was the only condition WikiLeaks would try to impose on us; what we wrote about the material was entirely up to us. . . .

We were confident that reporting on the secret documents could be done within the law, but we speculated about what the government . . . might do to impede our work or exact recriminations.

Digging Through the Data

Back in New York we assembled a team of reporters, data experts and editors and quartered them in an out-of-the-way office. Andrew Lehren, of our computer-assisted-reporting unit, did the first cut, searching terms on his own or those suggested by other reporters, compiling batches of relevant documents and summarizing the contents. We assigned reporters to specific areas in which they had expertise and gave them password access to rummage in the data. This became the routine we would follow with subsequent archives.

An air of intrigue verging on paranoia permeated the project, perhaps understandably, given that we were dealing with a mass of classified material and a source who acted like a fugitive, changing crash pads, e-mail addresses and cellphones frequently. We used encrypted Web sites. Reporters exchanged notes via Skype, believing it to be somewhat less vulnerable to eavesdropping. On conference calls, we spoke in amateurish code. Assange was always "the source." The latest data drop was "the package." When I left New York for two weeks to visit bureaus in Pakistan and Afghanistan, where we assume that communications may be monitored, I was not to be copied on message traffic about the project. I never imagined that any of this would defeat a curious snoop from the National Security Agency or Pakistani intelligence. And I was never entirely sure whether that prospect made me more nervous than the cyberwiles of WikiLeaks itself. At a point when relations between the news organizations and WikiLeaks were rocky, at least three people associated with this project had inexplicable activity in their e-mail that suggested someone was hacking into their accounts.

From consultations with our lawyers, we were confident that reporting on the secret documents could be done within the law, but we speculated about what the government—or some other government—might do to impede our work or exact recriminations. And, the law aside, we felt an enormous moral and ethical obligation to use the material responsibly. While we assumed we had little or no ability to influence what WikiLeaks did, let alone what would happen once this material was loosed in the echo chamber of the blogosphere, that did not free us from the need to exercise care in our own journalism. From the beginning, we agreed that in our articles and in any documents we published from the secret archive, we would excise material that could put lives at risk.

Redaction Procedures

Guided by reporters with extensive experience in the field, we redacted the names of ordinary citizens, local officials, activists, academics and others who had spoken to American soldiers or diplomats. We edited out any details that might reveal ongoing intelligence-gathering operations, military tactics or locations of material that could be used to fashion terrorist weapons. Three reporters with considerable experience of handling military secrets—Eric Schmitt, Michael Gordon and C.J. Chivers—went over the documents we considered posting. Chivers, an ex-Marine who has reported for us from several battlefields, brought a practiced eye and cautious judgment to the business of redaction. If a dispatch noted that Aircraft A left Location B at a certain time and arrived at Location C at a certain time, Chivers edited it out on the off chance that this could teach enemy forces something useful about the capabilities of that aircraft.

The first articles in the project, which we called the War Logs, were scheduled to go up on the Web sites of *The Times, The Guardian* and *Der Spiegel* on Sunday, July 25. We approached the White House days before that to get its reaction to the huge breach of secrecy as well as to specific articles we planned to write—including a major one about Pakistan's ambiguous role as an American ally. . . .

Three Papers Publish Simultaneously

We posted the articles on NYTimes.com the next day at 5 p.m.—a time picked to reconcile the different publishing schedules of the three publications. I was proud of what a crew of great journalists had done to fashion coherent and instructive reporting from a jumble of raw field reports, mostly composed in a clunky patois of military jargon and acronyms. The reporters supplied context, nuance and skepticism. There was much in that first round of articles worth reading, but my favorite single piece was one of the simplest. Chivers gathered all of the dispatches related to a single, remote, beleaguered American military outpost and stitched them together into a heartbreaking narrative. The dispatches from this outpost represent in miniature the audacious ambitions, gradual disillusionment and ultimate disappointment that Afghanistan has dealt to occupiers over the centuries.

If anyone doubted that the three publications operated independently, the articles we posted that day made it clear that we followed our separate muses. *The Guardian*, which is an openly left-leaning newspaper, used the first War Logs to emphasize civilian casualties in Afghanistan, claiming the documents disclosed that coalition forces killed "hundreds of civilians in unreported incidents," underscoring the cost of what the paper called a "failing war." Our reporters studied the same material but determined that all the major episodes of civilian deaths we found in the War Logs had been reported in *The Times*, many of them on the front page. (In fact, two of our journalists, Stephen Farrell and Sultan Munadi, were kidnapped by the Taliban while investigating one major episode near Kunduz. Munadi was killed during an ensuing rescue by British paratroopers.) The civilian deaths that had not been previously reported came in ones and twos and did not add up to anywhere near "hundreds." Moreover, since several were either duplicated or missing from the reports, we concluded that an overall tally would be little better than a guess. . . .

Assange was transformed by his outlaw celebrity.

Three months later, with the French daily *Le Monde* added to the group, we published Round 2, the Iraq War Logs, including articles on how the United States turned a blind eye to the torture of prisoners by Iraqi forces working with the U.S., how Iraq spawned an extraordinary American military reliance on private contractors and how extensively Iran had meddled in the conflict.

WikiLeaks Relationship Sours

By this time, *The Times*'s relationship with our source had gone from wary to hostile. I talked to Assange by phone a few times and heard out his complaints. He was angry that we declined to link our online coverage of the War Logs to the

WikiLeaks Web site, a decision we made because we feared—rightly, as it turned out—that its trove would contain the names of low-level informants and make them Taliban targets. "Where's the respect?" he demanded. "Where's the respect?" Another time he called to tell me how much he disliked our profile of Bradley Manning, the Army private suspected of being the source of WikiLeaks's most startling revelations. The article traced Manning's childhood as an outsider and his distress as a gay man in the military. Assange complained that we "psychologicalized" Manning and gave short shrift to his "political awakening."

The final straw was a front-page profile of Assange by John Burns and Ravi Somaiya, published Oct. 24, that revealed fractures within WikiLeaks, attributed by Assange's critics to his imperious management style. Assange denounced the article to me, and in various public forums, as "a smear."

Assange was transformed by his outlaw celebrity. . . .

New Conditions for Sharing Data

In October, WikiLeaks gave *The Guardian* its third archive, a quarter of a million communications between the U.S. State Department and its outposts around the globe. This time, Assange imposed a new condition: *The Guardian* was not to share the material with *The New York Times*. Indeed, he told *Guardian* journalists that he opened discussions with two other American news organizations—*The Washington Post* and the McClatchy chain—and intended to invite them in as replacements for *The Times*. He also enlarged his recipient list to include *El País*, the leading Spanish-language newspaper.

The Guardian was uncomfortable with Assange's condition. By now the journalists from *The Times* and *The Guardian* had a good working relationship. *The Times* provided a large American audience for the revelations, as well as access to the U.S. government for comment and context. And given the potential legal issues and public reaction, it was good to have company in the trenches. Besides, we had come to believe that Assange was losing control of his stockpile of secrets. An independent journalist, Heather Brooke, had obtained material from a WikiLeaks dissident and joined in a loose alliance with *The Guardian*. Over the coming weeks, batches of cables would pop up in newspapers in Lebanon, Australia and Norway. David Leigh, *The Guardian*'s investigations editor, concluded that these rogue leaks released *The Guardian* from any pledge, and he gave us the cables.

> *Because of the range of the material and the very nature of diplomacy, the embassy cables were bound to be more explosive than the War Logs.*

Assange Unhinged

On Nov. 1 [2010], Assange and two of his lawyers burst into Alan Rusbridger's office, furious that *The Guardian* was asserting greater independence and suspicious that *The Times* might be in possession of the embassy cables. Over the course of an eight-hour meeting, Assange intermittently raged against *The Times*—especially over our front-page profile—while *The Guardian* journalists tried to calm him. In midstorm, Rusbridger called me to report on Assange's grievances and relay his demand for a front-page apology in *The Times*. Rusbridger knew that this was a nonstarter, but he was buying time for the tantrum to subside. In the end, both he and Georg Mascolo, editor in chief of *Der Spiegel*, made clear that they intended to continue their collaboration with *The Times*; Assange could take it or leave it. Given that we already had all of the documents, Assange had little choice. Over the next two days, the news organizations agreed on a timetable for publication.

The following week, we sent Ian Fisher, a deputy foreign editor who was a principal coordinator on our processing of the embassy cables, to London to work out final details. The meeting went smoothly, even after Assange arrived. "Freakishly good behavior," Fisher e-mailed me afterward. "No yelling or crazy mood swings." But after dinner, as Fisher was leaving, Assange smirked and offered a parting threat: "Tell me, are you in contact with your legal counsel?" Fisher replied that he was. "You had better be," Assange said.

Fisher left London with an understanding that we would continue to have access to the material. But just in case, we took out a competitive insurance policy. We had Scott Shane, a Washington correspondent, pull together a long, just-in-case article summing up highlights of the cables, which we could quickly post on our Web site. If WikiLeaks sprang another leak, we would be ready.

The Impact of the Embassy Cables

Because of the range of the material and the very nature of diplomacy, the embassy cables were bound to be more explosive than the War Logs. Dean Baquet, our Washington bureau chief, gave the White House an early warning on Nov. 19. The following Tuesday, two days before Thanksgiving, Baquet and two colleagues were invited to a windowless room at the State Department, where they encountered an unsmiling crowd. Representatives from the White House, the State Department, the Office of the Director of National Intelligence, the C.I.A. [Central Intelligence Agency], the Defense Intelligence Agency, the F.B.I. [Federal Bureau of Investigation] and the Pentagon gathered around a conference table. Others, who never identified themselves, lined the walls. A solitary note-taker tapped away on a computer.

The meeting was off the record, but it is fair to say the mood was tense. Scott Shane, one reporter who participated in the meeting, described "an undertone of suppressed outrage and frustration."

Subsequent meetings, which soon gave way to daily conference calls, were more businesslike. Before each discussion, our Washington bureau sent over a batch of specific cables that we intended to use in the coming days. They were circulated to regional specialists, who funneled their reactions to a small group at State, who came to our daily conversations with a list of priorities and arguments to back them up. We relayed the government's concerns, and our own decisions regarding them, to the other news outlets.

Addressing the Government's Concerns

The administration's concerns generally fell into three categories. First was the importance of protecting individuals who had spoken candidly to American diplomats in oppressive countries. We almost always agreed on those and were grateful to the government for pointing out some we overlooked.

Even more than the military logs, the diplomatic cables called for context and analysis.

"We were all aware of dire stakes for some of the people named in the cables if we failed to obscure their identities," Shane wrote to me later, recalling the nature of the meetings. Like many of us, Shane has worked in countries where dissent can mean prison or worse. "That sometimes meant not just removing the name but also references to institutions that might give a clue to an identity and sometimes even the dates of conversations, which might be compared with surveillance tapes of an American Embassy to reveal who was visiting the diplomats that day."

The second category included sensitive American programs, usually related to intelligence. We agreed to withhold some of this information, like a cable describing an intelligence-sharing program that took years to arrange and might be lost if exposed. In other cases, we went away convinced that publication would cause some embarrassment but no real harm.

The third category consisted of cables that disclosed candid comments by and about foreign officials, including heads of state. The State Department feared publication would strain relations with those countries. We were mostly unconvinced. . . .

The Obama White House, while strongly condemning WikiLeaks for making the documents public, did not seek an injunction to halt publication.

A Need for Context

Even more than the military logs, the diplomatic cables called for context and analysis. It was important to know, for example, that cables sent from an embassy are routinely dispatched over the signature of the ambassador and those from the State Department are signed by the secretary of state, regardless of whether the ambassador or secretary had actually seen the material. It was important to know that much of the communication between Washington and its outposts is given even more restrictive classification—top secret or higher—and was thus missing from this trove. We searched in vain, for example, for military or diplomatic reports on the fate of Pat Tillman, the former football star and Army Ranger who was killed by friendly fire in Afghanistan. We found no reports on how [terrorist leader] Osama bin Laden eluded American forces in the mountains of Tora Bora. (In fact, we found nothing but second- and thirdhand rumors about bin Laden.) If such cables exist, they were presumably classified top secret or higher.

And it was important to remember that diplomatic cables are versions of events. They can be speculative. They can be ambiguous. They can be wrong. . . .

Striking a Balance Between Informing and Protecting

The tension between a newspaper's obligation to inform and the government's responsibility to protect is hardly new. At least until this year, nothing *The Times* did on my watch caused nearly so much agitation as two articles we published about tactics employed by the [George W.] Bush administration after the attacks of Sept. 11, 2001. The first, which was published in 2005 and won a Pulitzer Prize, revealed that the National Security Agency was eavesdropping on domestic phone conversations and e-mail without the legal courtesy of a warrant. The other, published in 2006, described a vast Treasury Department program to screen international banking records.

I have vivid memories of sitting in the Oval Office as President George W. Bush tried to persuade me and the paper's publisher to withhold the eavesdropping story, saying that if we published it, we should share the blame for the next terrorist attack. We were unconvinced by his argument and published the story, and the reaction from the government—and conservative commentators in particular—was vociferous.

This time around, the [President Barack] Obama administration's reaction was different. It was, for the most part, sober and professional. The Obama White House, while strongly condemning WikiLeaks for making the documents public, did not seek an injunction to halt publication. There was no Oval Office lecture. On the contrary, in our discussions before publication of our articles, White House officials, while challenging some of the conclusions we drew from the material, thanked us for handling the documents with care. The secretaries of state and defense and the attorney general resisted the opportunity for a crowd-pleasing orgy of press bashing. There has been no serious official talk—unless you count an ambiguous hint by Senator Joseph Lieberman—of pursuing news organizations in the courts. Though the release of these documents was certainly embarrassing, the relevant government agencies actually engaged with us in an attempt to prevent the release of material genuinely damaging to innocent individuals or to the national interest.

A free press in a democracy can be messy. But the alternative is to give the government a veto over what its citizens are allowed to know.

Mixed Public Reaction

The broader public reaction was mixed—more critical in the first days; more sympathetic as readers absorbed the articles and the sky did not fall; and more hostile to WikiLeaks in the U.S. than in Europe, where there is often a certain pleasure in seeing the last superpower taken down a peg.

In the days after we began our respective series based on the embassy cables, Alan Rusbridger and I went online to answer questions from readers. *The Guardian*, whose readership is more sympathetic to the guerrilla sensibilities of WikiLeaks, was attacked for being too fastidious about redacting the documents: How dare you censor this material? What are you hiding? Post everything now! The mail sent to *The Times*, at least in the first day or two, came from the opposite field. Many readers were indignant and alarmed: Who needs this? How dare you? What gives you the right?

Much of the concern reflected a genuine conviction that in perilous times the president needs extraordinary powers, unfettered by Congressional oversight, court meddling or the strictures of international law and certainly safe from nosy reporters. That is compounded by a popular sense that the elite media have become too big for their britches and by the fact that our national conversation has become more polarized and strident. . . .

Of Newspapers and Governments

I'm the first to admit that news organizations, including this one, sometimes get things wrong. We can be overly credulous (as in some of the prewar reporting about Iraq's supposed weapons of mass destruction) or overly cynical about official claims and motives. We may err on the side of keeping secrets ... or on the side of exposing them. We make the best judgments we can. When we get things wrong, we try to correct the record. A free press in a democracy can be messy. But the alternative is to give the government a veto over what its citizens are allowed to know. Anyone who has worked in countries where the news diet is controlled by the government can sympathize with Thomas Jefferson's oft-quoted remark that he would rather have newspapers without government than government without newspapers.

The intentions of our founders have rarely been as well articulated as they were by Justice Hugo Black 40 years ago, concurring with the Supreme Court ruling that stopped the government from suppressing the secret Vietnam War history called the Pentagon Papers: "The government's power to censor the press was abolished so that the press would remain forever free to censure the government. The press was protected so that it could bare the secrets of government and inform the people."

There is no neat formula for maintaining this balance. In practice, the tension between our obligation to inform and the government's obligation to protect plays out in a set of rituals. As one of my predecessors, Max Frankel, then the Washington bureau chief, wrote in a wise affidavit filed during the Pentagon Papers case: "For the vast majority of 'secrets,' there has developed between the government and the press (and Congress) a rather simple rule of thumb: The government hides what it can, pleading necessity as long as it can, and the press pries out what it can, pleading a need and a right to know. Each side in this 'game' regularly 'wins' and 'loses' a round or two. Each fights with the weapons at its command. When the government loses a secret or two, it simply adjusts to a new reality." . . .

Criticizing WikiLeaks

Beyond the basic question of whether the press should publish secrets, criticism of the WikiLeaks documents generally fell into three themes: 1. That the documents were of dubious value, because they told us nothing we didn't already know. 2. That the disclosures put lives at risk—either directly, by identifying confidential informants, or indirectly, by complicating our ability to build alliances against terror. 3. That by doing business with an organization like WikiLeaks, *The Times* and other news organizations compromised their impartiality and independence.

In the end, I can only answer for what my own paper has done, and I believe we have behaved responsibly.

I'm a little puzzled by the complaint that most of the embassy traffic we disclosed did not profoundly change our understanding of how the world works. Ninety-nine percent of what we read or hear on the news does not profoundly change our understanding of how the world works. News mostly advances by inches and feet, not in great leaps. The value of these documents—and I believe they have immense value—is not that they expose some deep, unsuspected perfidy in high places or that they upend your whole view of the world. For those who pay close attention to foreign policy, these documents provide texture, nuance and drama. They deepen and correct your understanding of how things unfold; they raise or lower your estimation of world leaders. For those who do not follow these subjects as closely, the stories are an opportunity to learn more. If a project like this makes readers pay attention, think harder, understand more clearly what is being done in their name, then we have performed a public service. And that does not count the impact of these revelations on the people most touched by them. WikiLeaks cables in which American diplomats recount the extravagant corruption of Tunisia's rulers helped fuel a popular uprising that has overthrown the government.

Risks of Data Are Real

As for the risks posed by these releases, they are real. WikiLeaks's first data dump, the publication of the Afghanistan War Logs, included the names of scores of Afghans that *The Times* and other news organizations had carefully purged from our own coverage. Several news organizations, including ours, reported this dangerous lapse, and months later a Taliban spokesman claimed that Afghan insurgents had been perusing the WikiLeaks site and making a list. I anticipate, with dread, the day we learn that someone identified in those documents has been killed.

WikiLeaks was roundly criticized for its seeming indifference to the safety of those informants, and in its subsequent postings it has largely followed the example of the news organizations and redacted material that could get people jailed or killed. Assange described it as a "harm minimization" policy. In the case of the Iraq war documents, WikiLeaks applied a kind of robo-redaction software that stripped away names (and rendered the documents almost illegible). With the embassy cables, WikiLeaks posted mostly documents that had already been redacted by *The Times* and its fellow news organizations. And there were instances in which WikiLeaks volunteers suggested measures to enhance the protection of innocents. For example, someone at WikiLeaks noticed that if the redaction of a phrase revealed the exact length of the words, an alert foreign security service might match the number of letters to a name and affiliation and thus identify the source. WikiLeaks advised everyone to substitute a dozen uppercase X's for each redacted passage, no matter how long or short.

Julian Assange has been heard to boast that he served as a kind of puppet master, recruiting several news organizations, forcing them to work in concert and choreographing their work.

Whether WikiLeaks's "harm minimization" is adequate, and whether it will continue, is beyond my power to predict or influence. WikiLeaks does not take guidance from *The New York Times*. In the end, I can answer only for what my own paper has done, and I believe we have behaved responsibly.

Diplomatic Damage Was Minimal

The idea that the mere publication of such a wholesale collection of secrets will make other countries less willing to do business with our diplomats seems to me questionable. Even Defense Secretary Robert Gates called this concern "overwrought." Foreign governments cooperate with us, he pointed out, not because they necessarily love us, not because they trust us to keep their secrets, but because they need us. It may be that for a time diplomats will choose their words more carefully or circulate their views more narrowly, but WikiLeaks has not repealed the laws of self-interest. . . .

As for our relationship with WikiLeaks, Julian Assange has been heard to boast that he served as a kind of puppet master, recruiting several news organizations, forcing them to work in concert and choreographing their work. This is characteristic braggadocio—or, as my *Guardian* colleagues would say, bollocks. Throughout this experience we have treated Assange as a source. I will not say "a source, pure and simple," because as any reporter or editor can attest, sources are rarely pure or simple, and Assange was no exception. But the relationship

47

with sources is straightforward: you don't necessarily endorse their agenda, echo their rhetoric, take anything they say at face value, applaud their methods or, most important, allow them to shape or censor your journalism. Your obligation, as an independent news organization, is to verify the material, to supply context, to exercise responsible judgment about what to publish and what not to publish and to make sense of it. That is what we did.

WikiLeaks Prosecution Would Be "Chilling"

But while I do not regard Assange as a partner, and I would hesitate to describe what WikiLeaks does as journalism, it is chilling to contemplate the possible government prosecution of WikiLeaks for making secrets public, let alone the passage of new laws to punish the dissemination of classified information, as some have advocated. Taking legal recourse against a government official who violates his trust by divulging secrets he is sworn to protect is one thing. But criminalizing the publication of such secrets by someone who has no official obligation seems to me to run up against the First Amendment and the best traditions of this country. . . .

Did WikiLeaks Change Journalism?

Whether the arrival of WikiLeaks has fundamentally changed the way journalism is made, I will leave to others and to history. Frankly, I think the impact of WikiLeaks on the culture has probably been overblown. Long before WikiLeaks was born, the Internet transformed the landscape of journalism, creating a wide-open and global market with easier access to audiences and sources, a quicker metabolism, a new infrastructure for sharing and vetting information and a diminished respect for notions of privacy and secrecy. Assange has claimed credit on several occasions for creating something he calls "scientific journalism," meaning that readers are given the raw material to judge for themselves whether the journalistic write-ups are trustworthy. But newspapers have been publishing texts of documents almost as long as newspapers have existed—and ever since the Internet eliminated space restrictions, we have done so copiously.

Nor is it clear to me that WikiLeaks represents some kind of cosmic triumph of transparency. If the official allegations are to be believed, most of WikiLeaks's great revelations came from a single anguished Army private—anguished enough to risk many years in prison. It's possible that the creation of online information brokers like WikiLeaks and OpenLeaks, a breakaway site announced in December [2010] by a former Assange colleague named Daniel Domscheit-Berg, will be a lure for whistle-blowers and malcontents who fear being caught consorting directly with a news organization like mine. But I suspect we have not reached a state of information anarchy. At least not yet.

4

WikiLeaks Is an Abuse of Internet Freedom

Pablo García-Mexía

Pablo García-Mexía is a visiting professor of Internet law at the College of William and Mary in Virginia. He is the chair of Internet law and government at the Universidad Internacional de La Rioja in Spain and is co-founder of Syntagma: Center of Strategic Studies, a private think tank specializing in Internet, legal, and good governance issues.

The very nature of the Internet means it is free from the constraints of traditional publishing, whether related to space, economics, politics, ideologies, or professional protocols and standards. The Web furthers the principles of liberty and has become a key factor in promoting civil and human rights around the globe. It is exactly because of these conditions that WikiLeaks was able to make sensitive classified documents public with little interference. But just because one can *do something, it doesn't mean that one* should. *WikiLeaks has done the Internet a huge disservice by overstepping the bounds of what can and should reasonably be published online. Up until now, the Internet has operated on the foundation of net neutrality, or extremely limited regulation and external interference. The WikiLeaks situation lends credibility to those who would like change that, and it may well be the excuse some governments have waited for to step in and finally regulate the Internet.*

If in any facet of life, freedom is crucial, so is the case on the Internet. It cannot be otherwise. To the said basis of plain common sense two others should be added, both peculiar to the Network of networks. One of them, the fact that the Internet has been designed precisely for that purpose, that of being a network free from all constraints, both to its technical standards and protocols, and to its contents. Freedom as against obstacles of all kinds, political, ideological or economic. This is the essence of a principle consequently inherent to the Internet, from its very inception called "end-to-end" and more recently known as the principle of Net neutrality.

> *Authoritative voices have enthusiastically saluted the leakage, with the indisputable argument that henceforth, no government can beforehand exclude the possibility that any of their activities may be disclosed in the future.*

The second reason is that the Internet has slowly but unceasingly become a whole new battleground for human and civil rights. Although this is due to many reasons, a very important one is the growing presence of the Internet in practically every field of human life. Clearly, if online initiatives like WikiLeaks have been possible this is precisely because of these principles of liberty. In the past, the information that WikiLeaks has now published on the sole basis of the Internet would have been, at best, held by certain media, which would have weighed warily its eventual release, according to the always intricate webs of interests in which they operate. Let us remember the tortuous process that followed the gradual publication by the *Washington Post* of reports on the Watergate affair [political scandal in 1972–74 caused by illegal and improper campaign activities], to name but one example.

WikiLeaks, by contrast, has had access to documents of great importance for international relations and domestic politics of many states in the world, including some as significant as the U.S. And unlike in older times, the Internet's echo has made it possible to spread them across the globe within hours.

Consider the Documents

Documents obtained by the way, through methods allegedly contrary to American laws, if only for the fact that the official having apparently leaked them was bound by a legal duty of confidentiality. Documents which, in some particularly sensitive cases, can compromise the security and defense of the U.S. and of Western nations in general, particularly as a result of public exposure of government vulnerabilities toward threats as serious as that of jihadist terrorism, for example.

Knowing that any document is bound to be made public at an inconvenient time, no government unit will risk reflecting in writing potentially controversial views.

Documents that after the leakage will derive in huge profits, either directly for those who obtained them in the first instance, or indirectly, for those "traditional" media that have edited them under the WikiLeaks "license". . . Authoritative voices have enthusiastically saluted the leakage, with the indisputable argument that henceforth, no government can beforehand exclude the possibility that any of their activities may be disclosed in the future. There is no doubt that transparency is an essential pattern of good governance, both at promoting the dissemination of achievements and the discovery of malpractices in the exercise of power. A different thing is however that this principle should not be balanced, even limited, against substantial goods of a perfectly comparable nature, as is defense and security in democratic states.

True: security and defense cannot turn into a "fig leaf" of indiscriminate protection to any governmental activities and their documentary counterparts. Hence the need to restrict secrecy in government to truly justified circumstances, to the extent that disclosure would endanger the life or comparable rights of persons or the very subsistence of the community itself. The fact is that the laws of democratic countries, and particularly their courts, have traditionally embraced these principles as of right.

This makes other arguments used to justify the actions of the now famous Julian Assange even more difficult to sustain. Among them that according to which the security of government executives or cabinets does not constitute any obligation to those who are publishing these documents. No one disputes that the security of more than one cabinet may have been compromised by WikiLeaks' actions, the problem is that the security of entire governments and also their populations has been jeopardized along the way. It is obvious that Western societies, in times like these, cannot give up that fundamental purpose of government. It can however be argued that not all the leaked documents have an impact on security or defense. And nothing could be objected in this regard, inasmuch as the disclosure does not concern documents having been previously classified as confidential by the relevant government.

A Compromising Possibility

According to this, should the same consideration be therefore extended in order to cover those documents which, although previously classified as confidential, have no impact on security and defense? I believe not, unless we want to neutralize any possibility for governments to make decisions freely on any issues of domestic or foreign policy. Knowing that any document is bound to be made public at an inconvenient time, no government unit will risk reflecting in writing potentially controversial views. Thus not only sincerity, but also efficiency will suffer. Saved all distances, in private life there are things, often unpleasant, that simply cannot be said, no matter how true they may be, and precisely because of that; this is also the case with government action: Let's face it, what head of state would speak in the same terms with their counterpart in a neighboring country, and also with their prime or foreign minister during the negotiation of a matter of mutual interest?

It is furthermore worthy of attention that those who so joyfully undermine some basic principles of coexistence in our democracies, simultaneously adhere to those principles which favor them, such as profit, in a cynical exercise of social parasitism. A new sample, very important indeed, of the nefarious "Anything goes" [sociologist] Ralf Dahrendorf wrote about? Very likely. In any case, without a doubt, an abuse of the freedom that, to a respectable extent, almost only the West has to offer. And a misuse of the reflection of that freedom on the Internet: net neutrality. We have seen what may end up being the consequences. It only remains to add that which, in relation to the Internet, is certainly the most serious: The Internet has flourished and triumphed in our societies, and thus has led to progress in them, thanks to that same freedom, thanks to its being a medium subject to extremely limited doses of regulation and external interference.

Nothing could be more wished by those governments, businesses or any other kind of institutions intending to curtail Internet freedom, than a relevant and intemperate enough conduct to justify their desire to intervene. Hopefully we can prevent that WikiLeaks will become that excuse.

5

WikiLeaks Is Not a Threat to National Security

Mark Stephens, interviewed by Emily Badger

Emily Badger is a Washington, D.C., correspondent for Miller-McCune, a bimonthly print magazine, and Miller-McCune.com, a daily online news site. Mark Stephens is a British attorney who represents WikiLeaks.

According to WikiLeaks's British attorney, Mark Stephens, the claim that WikiLeaks endangered American national security when it made classified documents public online is unfounded. Despite concerns that releasing the information would cause a diplomatic disaster for the United States, Stephens questions whether it has really caused any long-term damage. Embarrassment, not harm, he argues, was the ultimate result of the leaks. Such an outcome underscores the belief of many that the government classifies far too much information to begin with. In accepting and publishing the information, WikiLeaks did exactly what journalism outlets have been doing for years: digging up secrets to hold the government accountable. The main difference is that Wikileaks's high-tech system allows information to be truly submitted anonymously, which protects both the source and WikiLeaks itself.

Mark Stephens, the British attorney for WikiLeaks founder Julian Assange, is traveling to the United States this week [May 2, 2011] for a debate hosted by Index on Censorship and the Columbia University Graduate School of Journalism on the impact of the whistle-blowing site for journalism, national security and government secrecy. . . .

The panel, chaired by Index's chief executive, John Kampfner, will also include investigative journalist and security services expert Andrei Soldatov; Emily Bell, director of the Tow Center for Digital Journalism; and *Washington Post* columnist Richard Cohen.

Ahead of the debate—and on the heels of WikiLeaks' latest release of hundreds of documents from Guantanamo [US military base in Cuba]—Stephens talked with Miller-McCune.com about the U.S. government's reaction to WikiLeaks, what the site's existence says about the problem of overclassification, and how the flow of official information will forever be changed in the new era of digital leaks.

Below is an edited transcript.

Interview with Assange's Lawyer

Miller-McCune: In what way has WikiLeaks permanently altered what you refer to in this debate as "the information war"?

Mark Stephens: The genius of Julian Assange was really to spot the gap in the market.

Traditional media has followed WikiLeaks to try and develop their own electronic drop boxes.

For years, traditional media have had the drop box where you can anonymously put a brown envelope to the newspapers, and many people have done that. But the problem with this [type of] whistle-blowing was that people are often able to identify the leaker by the documents, because many of the documents are now in a situation where governments put secret identification features into them, such as a zero or an 0 will be filled in on page 12, 13, 14, 15, depending on which personnel it was distributed to. That's a very basic idea, but there are similar kinds of things you can do so you can go back and track—if you ever get the document—who it came from.

What Julian did was he made an organization which was stateless, and therefore, not as susceptible to the national laws in any individual state. He also made the organization international in the sense that a thousand people work with WikiLeaks around the world, and so if he becomes indisposed—as he was when he was in prison—for any length of time, there are many other people who can step in and did, and the organization carries on. He's got resilience built in. And as far as the person who is leaking is concerned, through his computer genius, he's been able to devise code which makes it impossible for the person receiving the electronic files to know who sent them.

This is incredibly important, as documents which are given to journalists [today] tend to come in CDs full of material, rather than the old-fashioned folders of documents. The material is downloaded from computers, it's a lot more material, a lot more to digest. From that perspective, you've got a sea change in the way in which information is flowing to the media. And of course, what has happened is it's obviously been successful by the very fact that traditional media has followed WikiLeaks to try and develop their own electronic drop boxes.

Assessing the Impact

Do we have to wait for the legal limbo around WikiLeaks—and the U.S. government's criminal investigation into it—to be resolved before we truly know the impact the site will have in the long run on how the media operates?

It's fair to say we don't know the full ramifications, but I think what we can say is that the government reaction has been to clamp down on leakers. There has been a sharp increase in the seeking out and threats to whistle-blowers, and people who have whistle-blown have been prosecuted criminally. So there's an attempt to choke off the supply of information to the media. That is, of course, worrying for all media, whether traditional or otherwise, particularly somewhere like Washington—where leaking and counterleaking and briefing, particularly of confidential and secret material, is part and parcel of the oil that wheels Washington.

One of the other things that we can say [is] that there is an attempt at fairly crude forms of censorship, and those have taken two forms. One is the denial-of-service attack, which was launched against WikiLeaks repeatedly, and that, obviously, made it a bit more difficult for them to function. We also see economic censorship in the sense that many American credit card companies stopped dealing with WikiLeaks. Governments clearly have a remedy and a response, but it is at the moment taking fairly crude forms of censorship and attacks on whistle-blowers.

Concern for Whistle-blowers

In the Pentagon Papers [a leaked classified report about the Vietnam War that was published by The New York Times *in 1971] case, the Supreme Court established that the act of publishing leaked information is not in and of itself illegal. But what about the repercussions for the leaker himself?*

It is the government's job to keep its own secrets, and it is the media's job to be a check and balance on that.

I have thought about this fairly carefully, and I think it's a fairly harsh thing to say, but people who whistle-blow very often do so understanding that they are breaking the law. And the question is: What do you do about the whistle-blower? It seems to me that clearly the media must do everything it can to protect the identity of the whistle-blower. One of the calculations that the whistle-blower makes when deciding whether to blow the whistle is: 1) How important is this? and 2) Am I going to get caught?

One of the factors in that is: Will the media give me up? If they are outed, if they are identified through traditional police work, or even through the assistance of the media, then in those circumstances, that person has to understand that they've broken the law, and they must take the consequences. There's a further calculation they're making, which is to say, effectively, if you break the law, your defense is actually in the court of public opinion. You make the judgment that the issue about which you are leaking to the public is of such moment that the public will be appalled and outraged, and that will be your defense—that [the government] will not prosecute you as a result.

Is the government entitled to keep any of its secrets?

It is the government's job to keep its own secrets, and it is the media's job to be a check and balance on that. For myself, clearly I would accept that the government must have its secrets. But as Richard Dearlove, the former head of MI6, has said, the state should have its secrets, but not as many, and not for as long as most people think. That's the critical factor.

> The dysfunctional nature of freedom of information, the overclassification, means that people are not going to stand for that lack of accountability in government.

Most right-thinking people would say yes, of course [information that would endanger lives or harm anti-terror operations] should be secret. But I have to say, I think it is shameful that 50 years on from the Bay of Pigs invasion in April of '61, the CIA has blocked the release of the official history of that disaster. This is nothing short of holding history for ransom while it is politically expedient to do so. A soldier who took part in that, or an activist who took part, who was 20 at the time would now be 70. The plans for that invasion have long since lost any sensitivity, and there's no reason why those documents should not be in the public domain.

Freedom of Information

Is there a direct relationship between a flawed freedom-of-information system like the one you've just described and the rise of whisteblowing outlets like WikiLeaks?

Freedom of information has been a good thing since 1766 when the Swedes first passed a freedom-of-information law. The theory in democratic society is that we know all things of moment so that we can make up our minds about the issues of the day. If we're not told most of the important matters on which to base our decisions, then clearly they're going to be skewed. If you have a freedom-of-information system which is defective, if you have an exponential increase in classification like we've seen in the last two to five years, where the classification graph goes up virtually vertically, at that point, you are going to see far more people whose consciences are going to be pricked to become whistle-blowers. The dysfunctional nature of freedom of information, the overclassification, means that people are not going to stand for that lack of accountability in government.

Do you think the distinction matters—as some people have suggested that it does—whether WikiLeaks was a passive recipient of the documents it leaked, or an active party in encouraging sources to break the law and leak them?

To some extent, journalists have to expect that the full, unvarnished ways in which they do business are now going to come under some public scrutiny. Every single news organization, every single security correspondent, every single journalist who has done any cutting-edge news reporting will have sources who have access to classified information, and they'll have classified information revealed to them. They will have said, in the course of conversations [with sources], "Actually, that's interesting, but we think there's an interesting story *here*," or "Do you have more on that particular subject?" In the overwhelming majority of cases, I think everybody around the world would recognize that as a normal journalistic endeavor. It's about seeking out the secrets; it's about holding the government accountable. It is not about counseling or procuring a crime, which is, I think, what people who have spoken of this have said. It's a normal part of journalism.

If we are to criminalize journalists because that's what they do, then you have to criminalize every journalist who has undertaken that, and that's an awful lot of them.

Mainstream Media Draws Distinctions

Some of the U.S. media outlets that have worked with WikiLeaks, such as The New York Times, *have been careful to draw a distinction between what they do (journalism), and what WikiLeaks does (providing information as a source). Is this a fair distinction?*

The first question I ask is: Why does it matter? In the U.K. [United Kingdom], it makes no matter whatsoever. So that's the first thing, but in America it may make a difference to shield laws. But it seems to me that [the distinction] fails to recognize that WikiLeaks is evolving and changing. When WikiLeaks first started, it was a pipe where people pushed information through it, and it appeared online. There was very little in intermediary activity. Now the documents that we see coming in are checked and verified, their authenticity is verified, there's quite a lot of work done in analyzing them, in putting them into context and background reporting. All of that seems to me to be a journalistic endeavor, an editorial endeavor.

Then you come back to the more prosaic descriptions of what is Julian Assange? Well, he's certainly a publisher. So are we saying that he doesn't get the protections of publishers?

Does that mean every person who owns a publishing house, like Rupert Murdoch [founder of News Corporation], is not entitled to these protections? I think clearly he is, clearly his editors are. And I think he's the editor-in-chief—he carries out the functions of an editor, and he also carries out the functions of a journalist. I think those, for me, are the real issues.

How do you think the U.S. government should have reacted to WikiLeaks?

I think the sensible reaction is probably the reaction I'm seeing from most senior [British intelligence] people. When they came to see me, they wanted to be reassured that nobody was going to be killed or going to be harmed, that that information was going to be redacted. Once we'd agree to that, [a security services official] said, well, of course, the Americans are the augers of their own misfortune.

We were told the diplomatic world would fall apart, and in fact, it hasn't. There's been embarrassment; there hasn't been disaster.

He said every other country in the world is not allowed to electronically copy to more than a thousand people any [classified] information whatsoever. And when they do copy information to that many people, he said, "we work on the assumption we're penetrated by the Russians, and Chinese, or anyone else. And so, of course, we put stuff in there for them, as they'd expect us to!" The fact that this [U.S.] information was copied to 2.5–3 million people tells you there was very little security. As the guy from the security services said, the only people who didn't know about this were the electorate.

Discomfort but No Real Harm

The second thing I would say is, about the protestation that there was going to be huge damage and harm, I suspect there was an uncomfortable weekend of a few calls, and at worst, the American ambassador to Libya had to be recalled because [Libyan dictator] Col. [Moammar] Gadhafi took exception to some of the rude things written about him. But has that done us any long-term harm? Would that man staying in Libya have done any difference?

We were told the diplomatic world would fall apart, and in fact, it hasn't. There's been embarrassment; there hasn't been disaster. The sensible, grownup thing to do would have been to understand this was probably a once-in-a-lifetime event; it is unlikely that this kind of electronic dump is going to recur, at least not in the immediate future.

I would have brought my electronic rules in line with every other proper country in the world, and at that point, I would have said, "OK, well, let's batten down hatches for a while and see how we ride this out." The American government can't have it both ways—to say this is going to be a cataclysmic disaster while at the same time saying to everybody, "We haven't learned anything new." Those two things are irreconcilable.

6

WikiLeaks Ensures Government Transparency

Julian Assange

Julian Assange is the founder and editor-in-chief of WikiLeaks.

WikiLeaks strongly self-identifies as a media organization whose mission is to keep governments accountable by fearlessly publishing facts that need to be made public. WikiLeaks practices "scientific journalism," in which readers may view the original source documents on which articles are based so that they can make up their own minds about the truth of a story. WikiLeaks has adopted new technologies to help it tell the truth in a new format, but the function of the organization is the same as other major media outlets. The media helps keep governments honest, and WikiLeaks's unique methods do much to ensure government transparency. The health of a democracy depends on the media being able to report things freely, and WikiLeaks is wrongfully being targeted for doing just that.

In 1958 a young Rupert Murdoch, then owner and editor of Adelaide's *The News*, wrote: "In the race between secrecy and truth, it seems inevitable that truth will always win."

His observation perhaps reflected his father Keith Murdoch's expose that Australian troops were being needlessly sacrificed by incompetent British commanders on the shores of Gallipoli. The British tried to shut him up but Keith Murdoch would not be silenced and his efforts led to the termination of the disastrous Gallipoli campaign.

Nearly a century later, WikiLeaks is also fearlessly publishing facts that need to be made public.

Democratic societies need a strong media and WikiLeaks is part of that media.

I grew up in a Queensland [Australia] country town where people spoke their minds bluntly. They distrusted big government as something that could be corrupted if not watched carefully. The dark days of corruption in the Queensland government before the Fitzgerald inquiry [a 1987 judicial inquiry into police corruption prompted by a local newspaper investigation] are testimony to what happens when the politicians gag the media from reporting the truth.

These things have stayed with me. WikiLeaks was created around these core values. The idea, conceived in Australia, was to use Internet technologies in new ways to report the truth.

Scientific Journalism Defined

WikiLeaks coined a new type of journalism: scientific journalism. We work with other media outlets to bring people the news, but also to prove it is true. Scientific journalism allows you to read a news story, then to click online to see the original document it is based on. That way you can judge for yourself: Is the story true? Did the journalist report it accurately?

Democratic societies need a strong media and WikiLeaks is part of that media. The media helps keep government honest. WikiLeaks has revealed some hard truths about the Iraq and Afghan wars, and broken stories about corporate corruption.

People have said I am anti-war: for the record, I am not. Sometimes nations need to go to war, and there are just wars.

But there is nothing more wrong than a government lying to its people about those wars, then asking these same citizens to put their lives and their taxes on the line for those lies. If a war is justified, then tell the truth and the people will decide whether to support it.

If you have read any of the Afghan or Iraq war logs, any of the US embassy cables or any of the stories about the things WikiLeaks has reported, consider how important it is for all media to be able to report these things freely.

Publishing in Good Company

WikiLeaks is not the only publisher of the US embassy cables. Other media outlets, including Britain's *The Guardian, The New York Times, El Pais* in Spain and *Der Spiegel* in Germany have published the same redacted cables.

Yet it is WikiLeaks, as the co-ordinator of these other groups, that has copped the most vicious attacks and accusations from the US government and its acolytes. I have been accused of treason, even though I am an Australian, not a US, citizen. There have been dozens of serious calls in the US for me to be "taken out" by US special forces. Sarah Palin [2008 Republican vice presidential candidate] says I should be "hunted down like [terrorist leader] Osama bin Laden", a Republican bill sits before the US Senate seeking to have me declared a "transnational threat" and disposed of accordingly. An adviser to the Canadian Prime Minister's office has called on national television for me to be assassinated. An American blogger has called for my 20-year-old son, here in Australia, to be kidnapped and harmed for no other reason than to get at me.

And Australians should observe with no pride the disgraceful pandering to these sentiments by [Australian Prime Minister] Julia Gillard and her government. The powers of the Australian government appear to be fully at the disposal of the US as to whether to cancel my Australian passport, or to spy on or harass WikiLeaks supporters. The Australian Attorney-General is doing everything he can to help a US investigation clearly directed at framing Australian citizens and shipping them to the US.

Prime Minister Gillard and US Secretary of State Hillary Clinton have not had a word of criticism for the other media organisations. That is because *The Guardian, The New York Times* and *Der Spiegel* are old and large, while WikiLeaks is as yet young and small.

Shooting the Messenger

We are the underdogs. The Gillard government is trying to shoot the messenger because it doesn't want the truth revealed, including information about its own diplomatic and political dealings.

Has there been any response from the Australian government to the numerous public threats of violence against me and other WikiLeaks personnel? One might have thought an Australian prime minister would be defending her citizens against such things, but there have only been wholly unsubstantiated claims of illegality. The Prime Minister and especially the Attorney-General are meant to carry out their duties with dignity and above the fray. Rest assured, these two mean to save their own skins. They will not.

Every time WikiLeaks publishes the truth about abuses committed by US agencies, Australian politicians chant a provably false chorus with the State Department: "You'll risk lives! National security! You'll endanger troops!" Then they say there is nothing of importance in what WikiLeaks publishes. It can't be both. Which is it?

It is neither. WikiLeaks has a four-year publishing history. During that time we have changed whole governments, but not a single person, as far as anyone is aware, has been harmed. But the US, with Australian government connivance, has killed thousands in the past few months alone.

United States Admits Harm Is Minimal

US Secretary of Defence Robert Gates admitted in a letter to the US Congress that no sensitive intelligence sources or methods had been compromised by the Afghan war logs disclosure. The Pentagon stated there was no evidence the WikiLeaks reports had led to anyone being harmed in Afghanistan. NATO [North Atlantic Treaty Organization] in Kabul [capital of Afghanistan] told CNN it couldn't find a single person who needed protecting. The Australian Department of Defence said the same. No Australian troops or sources have been hurt by anything we have published.

The swirling storm around WikiLeaks today reinforces the need to defend the right of all media to reveal the truth.

But our publications have been far from unimportant. The US diplomatic cables reveal some startling facts:

- The US asked its diplomats to steal personal human material and information from UN [United Nations] officials and human rights groups, including DNA, fingerprints, iris scans, credit card numbers, Internet passwords and ID photos, in violation of international treaties. Presumably Australian UN diplomats may be targeted, too.

- King Abdullah of Saudi Arabia asked the US to attack Iran.

- Officials in Jordan and Bahrain want Iran's nuclear program stopped by any means available.

- Britain's Iraq inquiry was fixed to protect "US interests".

- Sweden is a covert member of NATO and US intelligence sharing is kept from parliament.

- The US is playing hardball to get other countries to take freed detainees from Guantanamo Bay [US military base in Cuba]. [US President] Barack Obama agreed to meet the Slovenian President only if Slovenia took a prisoner. Our Pacific neighbour Kiribati was offered millions of dollars to accept detainees.

In its landmark ruling in the Pentagon Papers [a leaked classified report about the Vietnam War that was published by *The New York Times* in 1971] case, the US Supreme Court said "only a free and unrestrained press can effectively expose deception in government". The swirling storm around WikiLeaks today reinforces the need to defend the right of all media to reveal the truth.

7

WikiLeaks Is a Terrorist Organization

Declan McCullagh

Declan McCullagh is the chief political correspondent for CNET. He was previously a reporter for Time *and the Washington, D.C., bureau chief for* Wired.

WikiLeaks published classified information online that is being used by enemies of the United States, and thus, represents a clear and present danger to national security. Because of this, the US State Department should officially designate WikiLeaks as a terrorist organization. Doing so would give the United States several powerful ways to go after WikiLeaks, including cutting off its financial backing, seizing its assets, and making felons of anyone who contributes "material support" to the organization. In addition, WikiLeaks founder Julian Assange should be criminally charged under the Espionage Act for conspiracy to disclose classified information. Every possible legal means should be used to punish this security breach and ensure that WikiLeaks is not able to release more classified information that causes further damage.

The incoming chairman of the House Homeland Security Committee says WikiLeaks should be officially designated as a terrorist organization.

Rep[resentative] Peter King, the panel's presumptive next head, asked the [President Barack] Obama administration today to "determine whether WikiLeaks could be designated a foreign terrorist organization," putting the group in the same company as al-Qaeda and Aum Shinrikyo, the Japanese cult that released deadly sarin gas on the Tokyo subway [in 1995].

"WikiLeaks appears to meet the legal criteria" of a U.S.-designated terrorist organization, King wrote in a letter to Secretary of State Hillary Clinton reviewed by CNET. He added: "WikiLeaks presents a clear and present danger to the national security of the United States."

King's letter was prompted by a massive document dump totaling more than 250,000 State Department diplomatic cables, which WikiLeaks gave in advance to news organizations, including Germany's *Der Spiegel* and Spain's *El Pais*, and that began appearing on the Internet this morning [November 28, 2010]. The White House has condemned the release, which *Der Spiegel* called "nothing short of a political meltdown for U.S. foreign policy."

King also wrote separately to Attorney General Eric Holder, asking him to "criminally charge WikiLeaks activist Julian Assange under the Espionage Act" for conspiracy to disclose classified information. The Espionage Act makes it illegal to disclose "information relating to the national defense" if that information could be used "to the injury of the United States."

If the State Department adds WikiLeaks to the terror list, one effect would be to prohibit U.S. banks from processing payments to the group. WikiLeaks currently takes donations through PayPal, bank transfers, and Visa and Mastercard payments.

Punitive Measures

Another would be to trigger the punitive measures included in the Antiterrorism and Effective Death Penalty Act, which made it a federal felony to provide "material support or resources" to a terrorist organization. That would likely dry up support from U.S.-based volunteers for WikiLeaks—one volunteer has been detained and released at the border already—and curb the group's options for Web hosting services. (Both Wikileaks.org and Cablegate.WikiLeaks.org are currently hosted, in part, on Amazon.com servers in the United States.)

The news organizations have released a small subset of the cables. WikiLeaks itself says it has published only 220 of 251,287 of them and promises to post the rest "in stages over the next few months."

WikiLeaks has already been the target of often-strident denunciations from Washington officialdom.

That has, perhaps unintentionally, given critics in Washington's national security establishment a strong incentive to find a way to pull the plug on the document-leaking Web site as soon as possible, one way or another.

Connecticut Sen. Joe Lieberman, chairman of the Senate Homeland Security and Governmental Affairs Committee and a senior member of the Senate Armed Services Committee, said in a statement today: "I also urge the Obama administration—both on its own and in cooperation with other responsible governments around the world—to use all legal means necessary to shut down WikiLeaks before it can do more damage by releasing additional cables. WikiLeaks' activities represent a shared threat to collective international security."

Other Countries Consider Charges

Australia said today it's investigating whether today's release violated its laws (WikiLeaks editor Julian Assange has an Australian passport). And Sweden has issued an international warrant for Assange's arrest on sexual assault charges, which has been upheld by an appeals court. Assange denies the allegations.

WikiLeaks has already been the target of often-strident denunciations from Washington officialdom after releasing confidential military dispatches from Afghanistan and Iraq. *The Washington Times* and a former [George W.] Bush administration official suggested WikiLeaks as the first public target for a U.S. government cyberattack, and a Republican senator has proposed a law targeting WikiLeaks.

The Patriot Act increased the maximum penalties for violating what has become known as the "material support" law to 15 years in federal prison. In a 6-3 ruling this year [2011], the U.S. Supreme Court upheld that law as constitutional, saying the Draconian legal sanctions are reasonable "even if the supporters meant to promote only the groups' nonviolent ends."

If WikiLeaks is added to the State Department list, one problem for its supporters might be the relative vagueness of the term "material support." In a law review article, former UCLA [University of California, Los Angeles] chancellor Norman Abrams wrote that "the janitor or the pizza delivery person or a taxi driver, or anyone who provides the most mundane 'services,' would seem to be at risk of prosecution" if they could be said to know they're dealing with a designated terrorist group.

Update 11:20 a.m. PT [November 29, 2010]

Rep. Peter King appeared on MSNBC's "Morning Joe" this morning. Here's what he said when asked about the implications of declaring WikiLeaks to be terrorists:

King: Let me tell you, first of all, the benefit of that is we would be able to seize their assets and we'd be able to stop anyone from helping them in any way, whether it's making contributions, giving free legal advice, or whatever. It would also, I believe, strengthen the secretary of state's hand in dealing with foreign nations as far as trying to get them extradited, trying to get them to take action against them.

Either we're serious about this or we're not. And I know people may think this is a bit of a stretch, but I analogize this to the RICO [Racketeer Influenced and Corrupt Organizations] statute, where they had a pretty narrow definition of criminal enterprise in the beginning. By now that's been expanded quite a bit to deal with contemporary problems.

> *WikiLeaks and people that disseminate information to people like this are criminals, first and foremost.*

I think if we're going to live in this—in this world—in this technological world where information can be disseminated so quickly, we have to be serious and take firm, strong action against those who are putting American lives at risk. Because this will put people's lives at risk. [...]

[Joe] Scarborough: But you know you can't—you can't designate them a terror outfit.

King: Oh, Joe, I mean, we have to—I don't think we should write that off that quickly and say we can't do it. I mean, they are assisting in terrorist activity. The information they are giving is being used by al-Qaeda. It's being used by our enemies.

Update 5:30 p.m. PT [November 29, 2010]

The calls for an all-out campaign against WikiLeaks are growing more shrill. Tony Shaffer of the Center for Advanced Defense Studies, a former Defense Intelligence Agency officer, told Fox News that he would like to see military action against Assange: "I would look at this very much as a military issue. With potentially military action against him and his organization." (While the Obama administration no longer uses the term "enemy combatant," it claims the authority to "detain" someone who has provided "substantial support" to enemies of the United States.)

Update 6 p.m. PT [November 29, 2010]

White House press secretary Robert Gibbs today said: "WikiLeaks and people that disseminate information to people like this are criminals, first and foremost. And I think that needs to be clear." That's an indication the investigation has gone beyond WikiLeaks' source to the group itself. He added, when asked about legal action against WikiLeaks and Assange: "We are looking at a whole host of things, and I wouldn't rule anything out." And syndicated columnist Charles Krauthammer reportedly said on Fox News (I haven't seen this segment myself yet) that journalists should be investigated: "To say that if you are unlike CNN and *Wall Street Journal*, who apparently turned down collaboration with WikiLeaks, and you collaborate, we are going to look into possible prosecution."

Excerpts from King's Letter

Here are some excerpts from Rep. Peter King's letter to Secretary Hillary Clinton:

> I am writing to request that you undertake an immediate review to determine whether WikiLeaks could be designated a Foreign Terrorist Organization (FTO) in accordance with Section 210 of the Immigration and Nationality Act (INA). In addition, I urge you to work with the Swedish government to determine the means by which Mr. Julian Assange can be brought to justice for his actions while recognizing and respecting Swedish sovereign law.

> As Admiral Mike Mullen, Chairman of the Joint Chiefs of Staff, concluded, the "irresponsible posting of stolen classified documents by WikiLeaks puts lives at risk and gives adversaries valuable information." I concur with Chairman Mullen's statement. . . .

> From these acts, WikiLeaks appears to meet the legal criteria for FTO designation as (1) a foreign organization; (2) engaging in terrorist activity or terrorism which (3) threatens the security of U.S. nationals or the national security of the United States. Specifically, pursuant to Section 212(a)(3)(B) of INA (8 U.S.C. § 1182(a)(3)(B)) WikiLeaks engaged in ter-

rorist activity by committing acts that it knew, or reasonably should have known, would afford material support for the commission of terrorist activity.

We know terrorist organizations have been mining the leaked Afghan documents for information to use against us and this Iraq leak is more than four times as large. By disclosing such sensitive information, WikiLeaks continues to put at risk the lives of our troops, their coalition partners and those Iraqis and Afghans working with us. . . .

WikiLeaks presents a clear and present danger to the national security of the United States. I strongly urge you to work within the Administration to use every offensive capability of the U.S. government to prevent further damaging releases by WikiLeaks.

8

Wikileaks Should Be Prosecuted Under the Espionage Act

Dianne Feinstein

Dianne Feinstein is a Democratic senator from California and is chairwoman of the Senate Intelligence Committee.

WikiLeaks intentionally harmed the United States by releasing secret government documents that unquestionably damage national security and put lives at risk. WikiLeaks founder Julian Assange should be criminally charged with felonies under the Espionage Act of 1917. There is no doubt that both Assange's actions and his intent meet the criteria for violating the Act. Assange has stated publicly that he hopes WikiLeaks starts a social movement for revealing secrets to bring down governments, including the United States. Clearly, Assange is not a journalist; he is an outside agitator who wants to harm the United States. He should be prosecuted aggressively for espionage before he and his organization can do more harm.

When WikiLeaks founder Julian Assange released his latest document trove—more than 250,000 secret State Department cables—he intentionally harmed the U.S. government. The release of these documents damages our national interests and puts innocent lives at risk. He should be vigorously prosecuted for espionage.

The law Mr. Assange continues to violate is the Espionage Act of 1917. That law makes it a felony for an unauthorized person to possess or transmit "information relating to the national defense which information the possessor has reason to believe could be used to the injury of the United States or to the advantage of any foreign nation."

The Espionage Act also makes it a felony to fail to return such materials to the U.S. government. Importantly, the courts have held that "information relating to the national defense" applies to both classified and unclassified material. Each violation is punishable by up to 10 years in prison.

No doubt aware of this law, and despite firm warnings, Mr. Assange went ahead and released the cables on Nov. 28 [2010].

In a letter sent to Mr. Assange and his lawyer on Nov. 27 [2010], State Department Legal Adviser Harold Hongju Koh warned in strong terms that the documents had been obtained "in violation of U.S. law and without regard for the grave consequences of this action."

That he is breaking the law and must be stopped from doing more harm is clear.

Details of Koh's Letter

Mr. Koh's letter said that publication of the documents in Mr. Assange's possession would, at minimum:

- "Place at risk the lives of countless innocent individuals—from journalists to human rights activists and bloggers to soldiers to individuals providing information to further peace and security;

- "Place at risk on-going military operations, including operations to stop terrorists, traffickers in human beings and illicit arms, violent criminal enterprises and other actors that threaten global security; and,

- "Place at risk on-going cooperation between countries—partners, allies and common stakeholders—to confront common challenges from terrorism to pandemic diseases to nuclear proliferation that threaten global stability."

None of this stopped Mr. Assange. That he is breaking the law and must be stopped from doing more harm is clear. I also believe a prosecution would be successful.

In an October [2010] analysis of earlier WikiLeaks disclosures, the Congressional Research Service reported that "it seems that there is ample statutory authority for prosecuting individuals who elicit or disseminate the types of documents at issue, as long as the intent element can be satisfied and potential damage to national security can be demonstrated."

Both elements exist in this case. The "damage to national security" is beyond question. As for intent, Mr. Assange's own words paint a damning picture.

The disclosure of classified documents puts at risk our troops, law enforcement, diplomats, and especially the American people.

Intent Is Everything

In June [2010] the *New Yorker* reported that Mr. Assange has asserted that a "social movement" set on revealing secrets could "bring down many administrations that rely on concealing reality—including the U.S. administration." The same piece revealed Mr. Assange's stunning disregard for the grave harm his actions could bring to innocent people, which he dismisses as "collateral damage."

Mr. Assange claims to be a journalist and would no doubt rely on the First Amendment to defend his actions. But he is no journalist: He is an agitator intent on damaging our government, whose policies he happens to disagree with, regardless of who gets hurt.

As for the First Amendment, the Supreme Court has held that its protections of free speech and freedom of the press are not a green light to abandon the protection of our vital national interests. Just as the First Amendment is not a license to yell "Fire!" in a crowded theater, it is also not a license to jeopardize national security.

This latest WikiLeaks release demonstrates Mr. Assange's willingness to disseminate plans, comments, discussions and other communications that compromise our country. And let there be no doubt about the depth of the harm. Consider the sobering assessment, delivered in an email to employees of U.S. intelligence agencies late last month, by Director of National Intelligence James Clapper: "The actions taken by WikiLeaks are not only deplorable, irresponsible, and reprehensible—they could have major impacts on our national security. The disclosure of classified documents puts at risk our troops, law enforcement, diplomats, and especially the American people."

9

WikiLeaks Should Be Protected by Narrowing the Espionage Act

Laura Murphy and Michael Macleod-Ball

Laura Murphy is director of the American Civil Liberties Union (ACLU) Washington Legislative Office. Michael Macleod-Ball is the ACLU's legislative chief of staff and its First Amendment counsel.

The Espionage Act should not be applied to third-party publishers of classified information, such as WikiLeaks, because doing so would unconstitutionally infringe on the free speech rights of all Americans and have a chilling effect on investigative reporting and public discourse in this country. The Espionage Act is overly broad, and it should be revised to specifically protect publishers who have no involvement in the original leak of classified information and to limit the types of documents that can be classified in the first place. As one of America's cornerstone liberties, the First Amendment of the US Constitution plays a key role in maintaining a healthy democracy and must be vigorously defended. Congress should ignore pressure to expand the Espionage Act so that it can apply to publishers and should instead narrow the Act to protect the fundamental right of publishers—whether print or online—to gather and disseminate information freely without fear of criminal prosecution.

Laura Murphy and Michael Macleod-Ball, "The Espionage Act and the Legal and Constitutional Issues Raised by WikiLeaks." Written Statement of the ACLU before the House Judiciary Committee, December 16, 2010, pp. 1–7.

The American Civil Liberties Union (ACLU) commends the [House Judiciary] Committee and its staff for bringing attention to the Espionage Act and the legality of its proposed use against third-party publishers of classified information. If the Espionage Act were to be applied to publishers, it would have the unconstitutional effect of infringing on the constitutionally protected speech rights of all Americans, and it would have a particularly negative effect on investigative journalism—a necessary and fundamental part of our democracy. Application of the Espionage Act to publishers would compel individuals and journalists to refrain from publishing information that would be a valuable addition to today's marketplace of ideas. On behalf of the ACLU, a non-profit, nonpartisan organization having over half a million members, countless additional activists and supporters, and 53 affiliates nationwide, we urge Congress to resist the urge to broaden the Espionage Act's already overbroad proscriptions and, instead, to narrow the Act's focus to those responsible for leaking properly classified information to the detriment of our national security.

Instead of expanding the Espionage Act, Congress should limit its application and make the law more understandable.

What Is the Espionage Act?

The Espionage Act affords government a basis for prosecuting and penalizing, to the maximum possible extent, the improper leaking of classified information. In fact, the conduct proscribed by the Espionage Act is so broad that courts have been compelled to narrow the construction of certain terms in order to avoid finding the law unconstitutional. And still, media outlets—those responsible for informing the public and encouraging public discussion of important civic issues—remain at risk of prosecution under the Act. In the current environment, it would be all too easy for inflamed public passions to serve as the basis for arguments to justify broadening even further the proscriptions of the law. Instead, Congress should stand clear-eyed and firm against arguments based on passion, not reason—and narrow the Espionage Act to those who leak properly classified information. Publishers who are not involved in the leaking of classified information should be praised by our society for their contributions to public discourse, not vilified as the co-conspirators of leakers with whom they have no criminal connection.

Today's hearing is titled "Hearing on the Espionage Act and the Legal and Constitutional Issues Raised by WikiLeaks". Speculating about the facts underlying the recent WikiLeaks publications is less important than understanding the laws implicated by recent public discourse. The issues associated with the Espionage Act, even in its current form and without amendment as has been proposed, are extremely important to our democracy and go well beyond this one recent incident.

The federal government classifies far too much information, which damages national security and destroys government accountability and informed public debate.

Provisions Are Overly Broad

The Espionage Act has a long history and many flaws. Some of the law's provisions are breathtakingly broad. Read literally, some provisions would punish the transmission—by anyone, including organizations such as the *New York Times* or *Wall Street Journal*—of information that is unclassified and legitimately in the public sphere. Others would punish publication—again, by anyone—of information the release of which would have no negative impact on our national defense. Still others would punish publishers who are engaged in nothing more than well-understood norms of news gathering and dissemination. Some of these problems would be exacerbated by a recently introduced bill that purports to broaden the restrictions on information release.

Instead of expanding the Espionage Act, Congress should limit its application and make the law more understandable. While we urge restraint in applying the existing law in its current very broad form, if Congress is determined to act, we would urge Congress to take the following actions:

1. Improve the classification system to ensure that classified documents are properly classified.

2. Remove all references to 'publication' from the Espionage Act and limit prosecutions under the Act to those directly responsible for the improper acquisition or transfer of properly classified information.

Classification System Is Broken

Excessive government secrecy is not a new phenomenon. Nearly every entity commissioned to study classification policy over the last sixty years, from the Coolidge Committee in 1956 through the Moynihan Commission in 1997, has reached the same conclusion: the federal government classifies far too much information, which damages national security and destroys government accountability and informed public debate. Despite the results of these studies, reform has proven elusive and we are now living in an age of government secrecy run amok:

- According to the *Washington Post*, there are 1,271 government organizations and 1,931 private companies working on programs related to counterterrorism, homeland security and intelligence, and an estimated 854,000 people hold top-secret security clearances.

- According to the Information Security Oversight Office (ISOO), the government made 54,834,989 separate classification decisions in 2009 alone. ISOO changed the way it counted electronic records in 2009 so exact year-to-year comparisons are not possible, but this figure is more than double the record 23,241,098 classification decisions reported in 2008 and six times the 8,650,735 classification decisions made in 2001.

- Experts in security policy have estimated that at least fifty percent of the material the government classifies is made secret unnecessarily.

- "Derivative classification" in particular has exploded. Fully 99.66% of classification decisions are not made by the government's trained "original classification authorities" (OCAs), but by other government officials or contractors who may have received little or no training and wield a classification stamp only because they work with information *derived* from documents classified by OCAs.

- Document reviews conducted by ISOO discovered classification errors in 65% of the documents examined, with several agencies posting error rates of more than 90%. Errors which put the appropriateness of the classification in doubt were seen in 35% of the documents ISOO reviewed in 2009, up from 25% in 2008.

- Government agencies have been using a multitude of unregulated control designations to restrict the flow of *unclassified* information. Twenty federal government departments and agencies have used at least 107 different control markings with more than 131 different procedures for handling what those agencies considered "sensitive" information, with no legal justification.

The classification system in the United States is a mess. It is far too easy to classify documents and, as a result, thousands of documents are classified that, if released, pose no real risk to the national security. Documents that are unnecessarily classified under such a system have the effect of grossly expanding the penalties of the Espionage Act to the release and publication of documents having purely innocuous content—but which happen to be designated as secret. Such a system must be brought under control before the Espionage Act's provisions will have any semblance of fairness.

In a society where truth becomes treason, we are in big trouble.

Freedom of the Press

Freedom of the press is fundamental to our nation's identity and should be fiercely protected. From Watergate [political scandal in 1972–74 caused by illegal and improper campaign activities] to the warrantless wiretapping program, revelations of historic consequences are the product of a free and unrestricted press. At a time when those in power hide behind the phrase 'state secret' instead of 'no comment,' journalists should be commended for continuing to push beyond the hyperbole. In this regard, we must always distinguish between the actions of the source of properly classified information and the publisher of that information.

The state of our democracy is in peril when publishers are threatened with prosecution for treason and imprisonment and subpoenas are used as intimidation tactics. Americans found out about our government's use of warrantless domestic wiretapping only through intrepid reporting. Journalists cannot maintain their independence without access to information from confidential sources. More to the point, as Congressman Ron Paul recently said, "In a society where truth becomes treason, we are in big trouble."

Some Leaks Are Beneficial

While some leaked information can be seen by some as damaging to the national defense, many leaks have ultimately been viewed as shining a beneficial light on the workings of our government, outweighing any potential harm. The release of the Pentagon Papers [a leaked classified report about the Vietnam War that was published by the *New York Times* in 1971] during the time of the Vietnam War demonstrated the weakness in our decision making during that era and raised significant questions about the Gulf of Tonkin incident that served as the basis for putting the country on a more formal war footing. More recently, CIA [Central Intelligence Agency] secret prisons, the use of torture by US forces, and the practice of targeted killings by the United States all were disclosed through leaks to media outlets. The beneficial impact of such disclosures makes abundantly clear that a statute that could be read to permit prosecution for the release of all closely-held government information, regardless of whether it is properly classified, and regardless of its national defense impact, goes too far. In order to maintain our democratic values, commitment to free speech, and government accountability, not only should the classification system be repaired, but Congress should ensure the limitation of the Espionage Act so that it cannot be used to prosecute publishers with no involvement in the original leak of classified information.

The Medium of Media Shouldn't Matter

It is also worth noting in this discussion that the protections afforded publishers from prosecution ought not to be conditioned on the particular medium in which they happen to do their work. All publishers who engage in news gathering, research, writing, editing, audio or video recording, or other processes intended to obtain or produce information for public dissemination should be given equal status and are entitled to the protections of the First Amendment. The constitutional protections afforded publishers exist not in connection with any particular form of communication, but rather they are intended to stimulate the free flow of information in order to serve society's interests, including the need to hold government accountable and to acquire and share knowledge.

A law that criminalizes the reporting function of 'publication'—particularly when the publisher bears no responsibility for the underlying unlawful acquisition or transfer of secret information—does nothing but act in contravention of such principles. The medium is of no relevance in considering the merits of the constitutional right. Would the *New York Times* print edition carrying the Pentagon Papers have been treated differently by prosecutors than a mythical online version of the *Times* in the Vietnam era? Certainly, the answer is no and, at least as it relates to the current controversy, we should bear in mind that online publishers of news possess the very same protections as those in the traditional world of newspaper publishers and news broadcasters.

The First Amendment requires constant vigilance to protect against its erosion.

Uniform Standards Must Apply

And because the rights of online publishers and offline publishers are identical, any restrictions must be judged by the same standard. If we know anything about the rights of a free press and the right to free speech, it is that a restriction must be narrowly drawn to serve a compelling public interest. In the Pentagon Papers case, the government sought to bar publication of the released government documents and ultimately failed in that attempt. Can you imagine the outcry if the government sought not merely to stop publication of the Pentagon Papers, but also to shut down publication of the *New York Times* and *Washington Post* in full? Similarly, online publishers publish many things. If one published item is somehow deemed to be appropriately restricted, that determination in no way justifies taking an entire website down from the Internet. To do so would limit the exchange of information in the marketplace of ideas, would fail the 'narrow tailoring' test, and would fail to serve a compelling public interest.

As this Committee examines the Espionage Act, we urge the Committee to refrain from an emotional response in the wake of the most recent release of closely-held government information. Certain previous Congressional actions based upon inflamed passions have been detrimental to our democracy, and history has judged those actions harshly. The Alien and Sedition Acts were used to prosecute prominent Republican newspaper editors in the late 1700s. In the next century, similar laws were used to suppress the speech of abolitionists, religious minorities, suffragists, and pacifists. In the 1900s, laws were adopted against lecturing on birth control, labor organizing, and author Upton Sinclair was arrested for trying to read the text of the First Amendment. It was in response to these excesses that the American Civil Liberties Union was founded 90 years ago.

The First Amendment requires constant vigilance to protect against its erosion. It is designed to defend controversial speech and is rarely invoked to protect speech to which no one objects. The challenge for this Committee today and in the coming session is whether it will be able to engage in a sober assessment of the speech and press restrictions in the Espionage Act; and whether this Committee will be able to ensure that any new law it approves will be narrowly drawn so as to truly minimize its impact on the fundamental rights of free speech and a free press. To meet those challenges, this Committee and this Congress will surely need to narrow, not expand, the Espionage Act to take into account the wealth of improperly classified information, the wealth of classified information that does no harm to the national defense upon release, and the fundamental right of all publishers, whether on-line or off, to engage unrestrainedly in the traditional news gathering and dissemination process without fear of criminal prosecution.

10

WikiLeaks's Prosecution Would Imperil Freedom of the Press

James Goodale

James Goodale was legal counsel for The New York Times *in the Pentagon Papers case in 1971. He is currently working on a book titled* Fighting for the Press: Why the Pentagon Papers Case Still Matters.

In 1971, when The New York Times *published the infamous Pentagon Papers (a classified report about the Vietnam War that was illegally leaked to the paper), President Richard Nixon convened a grand jury and pushed to have the* Times's *reporter indicted for conspiracy to commit espionage. That effort failed, and so too should any indictment against WikiLeaks founder Julian Assange on the same basis. The courts have ruled that the First Amendment protects the media when it receives stolen information, as long as it did not help commit the crime. Just as the* Times *was protected during the Pentagon Papers case, so should WikiLeaks be protected now for publishing leaked war logs and diplomatic cables. If the WikiLeaks indictment proves successful, however, it will have a devastating effect on freedom of the press. Charging Assange with "conspiracy to commit espionage" would set a dangerous precedent that could more accurately be described as "conspiracy to commit journalism."*

Just in time to spoil the celebration of the 40th anniversary of the publication of the Pentagon Papers, the [President Barack] Obama Justice Department is trying to do what Richard Nixon couldn't: indict a media organization.

A grand jury investigation into WikiLeaks founder Julian Assange under the Espionage Act and the Computer Fraud and Abuse Act is underway in Alexandria, Virginia. The Justice Department has already subpoenaed the electronic records of many former WikiLeaks volunteers and at least three people have now been subpoenaed to testify in a case that could potentially criminalize forms of investigative journalism.

Many comparisons have been made between the Pentagon Papers and WikiLeaks, and most have focused on the landmark decision in *New York Times v. United States* that essentially banned prior restraints—or censorship orders—on the press. But long forgotten in Nixon's war on the press is an equally dangerous legal maneuver: Nixon convened a grand jury to indict the *New York Times* and its reporter, Neil Sheehan, for conspiracy to commit espionage—the same charge Obama's Justice Department is investigating Assange under today.

Pentagon Papers Victory Sets Precedent

In 1971, after Nixon had lost the Pentagon Papers case in the Supreme Court, he desperately wanted to bring criminal charges against *The Times*. Attorney General John Mitchell first went to U.S. Attorney Whitney North Seymour Jr. in New York and asked him to indict *The Times*. When Seymour refused, a grand jury was convened in Boston, where the prosecutors eventually dragged virtually every journalist and antiwar academic in the Cambridge [Massachusetts] area to court using subpoenas. The Justice Department wanted to know exactly who knew of the Pentagon Papers before they were released and how they ended up at the *New York Times*.

The government's "conspiracy" theory centered around how Sheehan got the Pentagon Papers in the first place. While [former defense analyst] Daniel Ellsberg had his own copy stored in his apartment in Cambridge, the government believed Ellsberg had given part of the papers to anti-war activists. It apparently theorized further that the activists had talked to Sheehan about publication in *The Times*, all of which it believed amounted to a conspiracy to violate the Espionage Act.

Grand Jury Testimony

Sheehan's wife, Susan, a reporter for *The New Yorker*, also was named in the government's case before the grand jury. A Who's Who of Boston-based reporters and anti-war activists were then forced to testify, including *New York Times* reporter David Halberstam, anti-war activists Noam Chomsky and two senatorial aides to Mike Gravel and Ted Kennedy. Harvard [University] Professor Samuel Popkin would even serve a week in jail for refusing to testify as to his sources, citing the First Amendment right to keep them confidential.

The First Amendment has long protected the transmission of information to journalists—even stolen information—as long as the journalist did not help commit the theft.

The grand jury investigation lasted more than a year and *The Times* was so sure Sheehan would be indicted that a statement was drawn up for *Times* Publisher Arthur Sulzberger that read in part, "The indictment of Neil Sheehan for doing his job as a reporter strikes not just at one man and one newspaper but at the whole institution of the press of the United States. In deciding to seek Mr. Sheehan's indictment, the administration in effect has challenged the right of free newspapers to search out and publish essential information without harassment and intimidation."

But thanks to the efforts of many First Amendment lawyers and the witnesses' outright refusal to testify as to their knowledge of the Pentagon Papers, this statement never had to be issued. The government was eventually forced to dissolve the grand jury once it became clear it would be impossible to indict.

Deja Vu All Over Again

The same scene is playing out in a grand jury room in Alexandria today. Julian Assange is being investigated for conspiracy to commit espionage for allegedly speaking with the purported leaker, Bradley Manning. Chat logs between Manning and FBI [Federal Bureau of Investigation] informant Adrian Lamo suggest the two did converse at one point, and if the logs are to be believed, they may have talked about the WikiLeaks disclosures.

Charging Julian Assange with "conspiracy to commit espionage" would effectively be setting a precedent with a charge that more accurately could be characterized as "conspiracy to commit journalism."

This, however, should not matter. Journalists communicate with sources all the time, regularly persuading them to leak. The First Amendment has long protected the transmission of information to journalists—even stolen information—as long as the journalist did not help commit the theft. Just as it protected Neil Sheehan in receiving the Pentagon Papers, it protects Julian Assange in receiving the WikiLeaks files, and neither should have to worry about being indicted for, as Sulzberger said, "doing their job as a reporter."

If an indictment and conviction of Assange were ever to be achieved, the courtroom scenes from that grand jury room 40 years ago could become commonplace. Not only would reporters be hauled in and questioned ("Did you write this to hurt U.S. foreign policy?" "Are you anti-war?"), but other reporters, not even assigned to the story, would be dragged in as well. Halberstam and the like did not have possession of the Pentagon Papers, but they were still subpoenaed just to find out if they knew who had them.

Charging Julian Assange with "conspiracy to commit espionage" would effectively be setting a precedent with a charge that more accurately could be characterized as "conspiracy to commit journalism."

11

WikiLeaks Shows the Need for a New Kind of "Watchdog" Protection

Jonathan Peters

Attorney Jonathan Peters is the Frank Martin Fellow at the Missouri School of Journalism, where he is working on his PhD and specializing in First Amendment issues. He has written on legal issues for a variety of news media and scholarly journals.

Although WikiLeaks disseminates information that adds to the public discourse, it does not thoroughly analyze and contextualize the information it publishes online. Because of this, it fails to meet the standard to claim the federal reporter's privilege, which protects journalists from being compelled by the courts to reveal sources or discuss unpublished information. WikiLeaks is a new type of media organization that does not fall into existing categories or roles, but it still plays an important role in the larger field of journalism. A new type of legal protection is needed for media "watchdog" organizations like WikiLeaks that collect information about matters of public concern and publish them without participating in the traditional newsgathering activities that bestow legal protection.

WikiLeaks makes news and shapes the public agenda. But the site, and any that follow in its footsteps, would be vulnerable if dragged into a U.S. federal court proceeding aimed at unmasking a source. Fifth Amendment protections aside, WikiLeaks wouldn't qualify to claim the federal reporter's privilege.

To make sense of that point, which I explain at greater length in this month's [May 2011] *Federal Communications Law Journal*, it helps to put the privilege in context. Journalists usually aren't exempt from laws that apply to the general public. They can't trespass to report a story, for example, and they can't steal documents. However, people who act as journalists can get special treatment in at least one way—invoking the reporter's privilege to refuse to testify about sources or unpublished information.

Although Congress has failed multiple times (as recently as last year) to codify the reporter's privilege in a statute, nearly all of the federal appeals courts have come to recognize the privilege in relation to the First Amendment. In doing so, they've struggled to resolve the threshold issue in those cases: Who qualifies to claim the privilege?

The Reporter's Privilege

The first and most important case to hit that issue head-on was *In re Madden*, decided in 1998 by the 3rd U.S. Circuit Court of Appeals. In a civil suit between two companies promoting professional wrestling, one of the people involved—a World Championship Wrestling commentator named Michael Madden—claimed the reporter's privilege during a deposition. Madden refused to identify any of his sources of information for the commentaries he read on the WCW's 900-number hotline.

The appeals court ruled that Madden didn't qualify for the privilege, and laid out a three-part test that's become the standard: Anyone claiming the privilege:

1. Must be engaged in investigative reporting.

2. Must be gathering news.

3. Must have had "the intent at the inception of the news-gathering process to disseminate the news to the public."

The court didn't fill in all of the blanks, but it did say the test "does not grant status [automatically] to any person with a manuscript, a web page or a film." Other federal courts, before and after Madden, have said the same thing and made clear that the medium doesn't determine whether someone can claim the privilege—a website is as valid a news vehicle as a newspaper.

WikiLeaks Faces *Madden* Test

Each prong in the *Madden* test is a hurdle for WikiLeaks to jump. Two of them wouldn't be problems, because the site's stated purpose is to disseminate information to the public, and its content is often newsworthy. The "investigative journalism" hurdle is the one that would trip up WikiLeaks.

Investigative journalism—according to journalism scholarship and a body of case law—involves more than dumping documents. It requires people to make an understandable story out of a mountain of information, to exercise editorial judgment, and to engage in analysis. Those activities are evident in the privilege cases around the country that followed *Madden*, and anyone engaged in those activities, journalist or not, can stake a claim to the privilege.

Even though WikiLeaks doesn't perform investigative journalism per se, it has a place in the larger ecosystem of journalism.

The courts should recognize a limited "watchdog privilege," invocable by anyone who collects information about matters of public concern for dissemination to the public.

But WikiLeaks largely has passed on to the traditional news media the burden of adding value to the leaked documents, of contextualizing them, and of explaining their meaning and significance. Aside from a few stories it published (which really were press releases) and the Collateral Murder video (which WikiLeaks edited and supplemented with interviews and storytelling), the site hasn't produced understandable, original stories out of the material it's released.

As a result, the WikiLeaks staff wouldn't qualify to claim the federal reporter's privilege.

But is that how things should be? I avoided that question in my journal article. But it's worth answering.

The Larger Landscape of Journalism

That's because, even though WikiLeaks doesn't perform investigative journalism per se, it has a place in the larger ecosystem of journalism. Newspapers, magazines and other outlets around the world have repeatedly, and to great effect, made use of WikiLeaks documents, most recently the files on Guantanamo Bay [US military base in Cuba] and the U.S. diplomatic cables.

The courts should recognize a limited "watchdog privilege," invocable by anyone who collects information about matters of public concern for dissemination to the public.

A reporter's privilege that excludes WikiLeaks while including the outlets that later use the leaked material is a bit irrational. It's like an electrical wire that burns up to protect a fuse.

There are two ways the courts could carve out a privilege that would cabin WikiLeaks and similar sites. They could reconceptualize what it means to do journalism, or they could devise a privilege that encompasses a wider array of communication activities. Because I'm not prepared to say that journalism involves anything less than editorial judgment, analysis and telling stories, I like the second idea.

Specifically, the courts should recognize a limited "watch-dog privilege," invocable by anyone who collects information about matters of public concern for dissemination to the public. I say "limited" because the privilege's backend would include all the garden-variety exceptions (e.g., testimony could be compelled where there is a direct, imminent threat to national security).

"Watchdog Privilege" Would Give New Protections

That approach is consistent with the general purpose of the reporter's privilege: to protect the free flow of information (not the institutional press) by ensuring that the government can't routinely conscript reporters as investigators. The worry is that the shadow of subpoenas discourages people from exchanging information.

The "watchdog privilege" is broad, sure, but not so broad that it's unworkable. It excludes purely private communication, which wouldn't contribute to the marketplace of ideas, and it requires that the content pertain to matters of public concern (e.g., information of broad interest about local, state, national, or world issues and events).

Although the privilege may put the courts in the dangerous position of deciding what's of broad interest, libel law does the same thing. Plus, the privilege recognizes that the Internet has created what Harvard law professor Yochai Benkler calls the "networked fourth estate." It combines elements of the "traditional news media with those of the new," based on decentralized information production.

Some of the players in that network engage in editorial judgment, analysis and telling stories; others do not. To the extent that they collect information about matters of public concern for dissemination to the public, they should qualify to claim the privilege. That includes WikiLeaks, however one feels about its actions in specific cases.

Organizations to Contact

The editors have compiled the following list of organizations concerned with the issues debated in this book. The descriptions are derived from materials provided by the organizations. All have publications or information available for interested readers. The list was compiled on the date of publication of the present volume; names, addresses, phone and fax numbers, and e-mail and Internet addresses may change. Be aware that many organizations take several weeks or longer to respond to inquiries, so allow as much time as possible.

American Civil Liberties Union (ACLU)
125 Broad St., 18th Floor, New York, NY   10004
(212) 549-2500
e-mail: info@aclu.org
website: www.aclu.org

Through activism in courts, legislatures and communities nationwide, the ACLU works to defend and preserve the individual rights and liberties that the US Constitution and laws of the United States guarantee everyone. The ACLU website has an extensive collection of reports, briefings, and news updates related to freedom of speech and expression in electronic media, including nearly a hundred that are specifically about WikiLeaks. Reports available on the ACLU website include "Pretending WikiLeaks Doesn't Exist: Government Secrecy Reaches Absurdity," "Free Speech Triumphs in WikiLeaks Case," and "Civil Liberties in the Digital Age."

Berkman Center for Internet and Society
Harvard University, Cambridge, MA   02138
(617) 495-7547 • fax: (617) 495-7641
website: http://cyber.law.harvard.edu

The Berkman Center for Internet and Society was founded to explore cyberspace, share in its study, and help pioneer its development. The center represents a network of faculty, students, fellows, entrepreneurs, lawyers, and virtual architects working to identify and engage with the challenges and opportunities of cyberspace. Its faculty, fellows, students, and affiliates engage with a wide spectrum of Internet issues, including governance, privacy, intellectual property, content control, and electronic commerce. The Berkman Center's Citizen Media Law Project (CMLP) and Cyberlaw Clinic joined a coalition of media and public interest organizations in filing an amici curiae (friend of the court) brief urging a federal district court judge to reconsider his orders shutting down WikiLeaks. The center's website includes news items, links, and frequent updates on the WikiLeaks case.

Center for Democracy and Technology (CDT)
1634 I St. NW, #1100, Washington, DC   20006
(202) 637-9800 • fax: (202) 637-0968
e-mail: www.cdt.org/contact
website: www.cdt.org

The Center for Democracy and Technology (CDT) is a nonprofit public interest organization that works to keep the Internet open, innovative, and free. As a civil liberties group with expertise in law, technology, and policy, CDT advocates for free expression and privacy in communications technologies by finding practical and innovative solutions to public policy challenges while protecting civil liberties. CDT is dedicated to building consensus among all parties interested in the future of the Internet and other new communications media. The CDT's "Global Policy Weekly" blog highlights the latest Internet policy developments and proposals from around the world, including WikiLeaks, and the CDT website features regular news updates on the WikiLeaks case.

Electronic Frontier Foundation (EFF)
454 Shotwell St., San Francisco, CA   94110-1914
(415) 436-9333 • fax: (415) 436-9993
e-mail: info@eff.org
website: www.eff.org

The Electronic Frontier Foundation (EFF) is an international nonprofit digital rights advocacy and legal organization. The group works to raise public awareness about civil liberties and computer-based communications, educate policymakers and the public about issues that underlie free and open communications, and support litigation in the public interest to preserve, protect, and extend First Amendment rights in the digital world. The EFF website features information about the group's various projects and initiatives as well as white papers, legal case documents, and press releases. Its regularly updated "Deeplinks" blog features posts on topics related to electronic communications, privacy, censorship, regulation, free expression, and activism. WikiLeaks-related material on the site includes copies of legal documents and statements submitted by EFF on WikiLeaks's behalf, and more than fifty blog posts that provide summaries of WikiLeaks news and analysis, and which links to the original material.

First Amendment Coalition (FAC)
534 4th St., Suite B, San Rafael, CA   94901
(415) 460-5060 • fax: (415) 460-5155
website: www.firstamendmentcoalition.org

Founded in 1988, the First Amendment Coalition (FAC) is a nonprofit public interest organization dedicated to advancing free speech, open and accountable government, and public participation in civic affairs. The Coalition acts locally, statewide, and nationally by offering free legal consultations for anyone frustrated in the exercise of their First Amendment rights; strategic litigation to enhance First Amendment freedoms; educational and informational programs offered online, in books, and in conferences; legislative oversight; and public advocacy through writings of Op-Eds and public speaking. The FAC website includes dozens of items related to WikiLeaks, including the essays "Unplug WikiLeaks? Enact a Federal Shield Law Instead" and "Will Mainstream Media Match WikiLeaks' Technology for Receiving Leaked Documents Anonymously and Securely? Not Likely." The FAC site also maintains an extensive law library of leading court decisions in the areas of freedom of information and freedom of speech, including the WikiLeaks case.

First Amendment Project (FAP)

736 Franklin St., 9th Floor, Oakland, CA   94612
(510) 208-7744 • fax: (510) 208-4562
e-mail: fap@thefirstamendment.org
website: http://thefirstamendment.org

The First Amendment Project is a nonprofit advocacy organization dedicated to protecting and promoting freedom of information, expression, and petition. It provides advice, educational materials, and legal representation to its core constituency of activists, journalists, and artists. Its website offers guides and handbooks that focus on legal issues, activism, and the process of gaining access to information. The site features extensive free speech and free press resources, as well as links to other organizations with similar goals.

Internet Society (ISOC)

International Secretariat, Reston, VA   20190
(703) 439-2120
website: http://internetsociety.org

The Internet Society is a non-governmental organization with more than twenty thousand members in one hundred eighty countries. Its members include groups responsible for the maintenance of the Internet's infrastructure and standards, including the Internet Engineering Task Force and the Internet Architecture Board. The Internet Society maintains a clearinghouse for Internet information and education. Its website includes an Internet Code of Conduct section, with documents covering topics such as ethics and the Internet. The society's formal position about WikiLeaks is available on its website as "The Internet Society on the WikiLeaks Issue."

New America Foundation

1899 L St. NW, Suite 400, Washington, DC   20036

(202) 986-2700 • fax: (202) 986-3696

website: www.newamerica.net

The New America Foundation is a nonprofit, non-partisan public policy institute that invests in new thinkers and new ideas to address the next generation of challenges facing the United States. New America supports municipal broadband and publishes articles and policy papers on the Internet. Its website features a variety of articles about WikiLeaks, including "Why the WikiLeaks Drama Is Overblown," "WikiLeaks, Amazon and the New Threat to Internet Speech," and "WikiLeaks: Diplomacy vs. Policy."

US Department of Justice (DOJ)

980 Pennsylvania Ave. NW, Washington, DC   20530-0001

(202) 514-2000

e-mail: AskDOJ@usdoj.gov

website: www.justice.gov

The Department of Justice (DOJ) is the federal executive department responsible for the enforcement of law and the administration of justice in the United States. The DOJ is led by the US Attorney General. The DOJ website offers press releases about its activities, including the 2011 announcement titled, "Sixteen Individuals Arrested in the United States for Alleged Roles in Cyber Attacks." The notice explains the arrest of a group suspected of conducting an electronic cyber-attack on the money-exchange website PayPal in retaliation for PayPal cutting off WikiLeaks's access to fundraising. If individuals associated with WikiLeaks are eventually arrested and face charges in the United States in connection with the classified documents published online by WikiLeaks, the DOJ website will provide detailed information about the DOJ's role in the case.

US Senate

Washington, DC 20510
(202) 224-3121
website: www.senate.gov

The US Senate is the upper house of the bicameral legislature in Washington, D.C. Along with the House of Representatives, it comprises the US Congress. One of the Senate's functions is to create bills and get them approved as laws by both houses of Congress. The US Senate's website includes more than fifteen hundred documents related to WikiLeaks, ranging from transcripts of Congressional testimony, statements about WikiLeaks by individual senators, news updates, and information about the many legislative efforts related to the WikiLeaks case.

WikiLeaks.org

website: www.wikileaks.org

WikiLeaks is a nonprofit electronic media organization that offers a secure and anonymous way for sources to share information. WikiLeaks then publishes the original source material alongside its news stories. Although the organization is enduring a financial embargo and having trouble staying afloat, as of press time, the WikiLeaks website was still functional and all of WikiLeaks's major published leaks were still available for download from the site in their entirety, including the Collateral Murder video, the Iraq and Afghanistan War Logs, and the US Embassy Diplomatic Cables.

Bibliography

Books

Julian Assange	*Julian Assange—The Unauthorised Autobiography*. Edinburgh, Scotland: Canongate Books, 2011.
Daniel Domscheit-Berg	*Inside WikiLeaks—My Time with Julian Assange at the World's Most Dangerous Website*. New York: Random House, 2011.
David Leigh and Luke Harding	*WikiLeaks: Inside Julian Assange's War on Secrecy*. London: Public Affairs, 2011.
Greg Mitchell	*The Age of WikiLeaks: From Collateral Murder to Cablegate (and Beyond)*. Los Angeles: Sinclair Books, 2011.
Greg Mitchell	*Bradley Manning: Truth and Consequences*. Los Angeles: Sinclair Books, 2011.
Sophie Radermecker and Valerie Guichaoua	*Julian Assange—WikiLeaks: Warrior for Truth*. Montreal, Canada: Cogito Media Group, 2011.
Micah Sifry	*WikiLeaks and the Age of Transparency*. Berkeley, CA: Counterpoint, 2011.
Alexander Star and Bill Keller	*Open Secrets: WikiLeaks, War and American Diplomacy*. New York: The New York Times, 2011.

Periodicals and Internet Sources

Esther Addley and Jason Deans — "WikiLeaks Suspends Publishing to Fight Financial Blockade," *The Guardian*, October 24, 2011.

Ben Adler — "Why Journalists Aren't Standing Up for WikiLeaks," *Newsweek*, January 4, 2011. www.thedailybeast.com.

Agence France-Presse (AFP) — "WikiLeaks Details Surveillance Industry," *Brisbane Times* (Australia), December 2, 2011. http://news .brisbanetimes.com.au.

Christopher Albon — "How WikiLeaks Just Set Back Democracy in Zimbabwe," *The Atlantic*, December 28, 2010.

C. Fred Alford — "Whistleblowing: Broken Lives and Organizational Power," *The New York Times*, December 9, 2010.

Alex Altman — "A Coming Chill Over Internet Freedom?" *Time*, February 20, 2008. www.time.com.

Associated Press — "PayPal Turns Off Tap for WikiLeaks Donations," CBS News.com, December 2010. www.cbsnews.com.

Associated Press — "Visa Says It Has Suspended All Payments to WikiLeaks 'Pending Further Investigation,'" *Star Tribune*, December 7, 2010.

B.G. — "More WikiLeaks—The 24-hour Athenian Democracy," *The New York Times*, December 8, 2010.

Henry Blodget   "WikiLeaks Spokesman Quits, Blasts
                         Founder Julian Assange as Paranoid
                         Control Freak, Admits to Using Fake
                         Name," *San Francisco Chronicle*,
                         September 28, 2010.

John Burns and   "WikiLeaks Founder on the Run,
Ravi Somaiya   Trailed by Notoriety," *The New York
                         Times*, October 23, 2010.

Massimo   "WikiLeaks' War on Secrecy: Truth's
Calabresi   Consequences," *Time*, December 2,
                         2010. www.time.com.

David Carr   "WikiLeaks Taps Power of the Press,"
                         The New York Times, December 12,
                         2010.

Hillary Rodham   "Remarks on Internet Freedom," US
Clinton   Department of State, January 21,
                         2010. www.state.gov.

Cornell University   "WikiLeaks Resources," 2011.
New Media and   http://blogs.cornell.edu/newmedia
Society Blog   andsociety2011.

Elizabeth   "The First WikiLeaks Revolution?"
Dickinson   *Foreign Policy*, January 13, 2011.

Economist   "Read Cables and Red Faces—Even
                         Those Who Back More Disclosure
                         Should Hesitate Before Condoning
                         WikiLeaks' Torrent of E-mails,"
                         December 2, 2010.

Anthony Faiola   "WikiLeaks Founder's Arrest in
and Jerry Markon   Britain Complicates Efforts to
                         Extradite Him," *Washington Post*,
                         December 7, 2010.

Megan Friedman   "Julian Assange: Readers' Choice for Time's Person of the Year 2010," *Time*, December 13, 2010. www.time.com.

Dave Gilson   "WikiLeaks Gets a Facelift," *Mother Jones*, May 19, 2010.

Todd Gitlin   "Everything Is Data, but Data Isn't Everything," *The New Republic*, December 7, 2010.

Andy Greenberg   "An Interview with WikiLeaks' Julian Assange," *Forbes*, November 29, 2010.

Glenn Greenwald   "The War on WikiLeaks and Why It Matters," *Salon*, March 27, 2010. www.salon.com.

Evan Hansen   "Why WikiLeaks Is Good for America," *Wired*, December 6, 2010.

Scott Horton   "Financing WikiLeaks," *Harper's Magazine*, August 6, 2010.

Andrew Keen   "When 'Anonymous' Protest Goes Too Far," CNN.com, December 11, 2010. http://articles.cnn.com.

Raffi Khatchadourian   "No Secrets: Julian Assange's Mission for Total Transparency," *The New Yorker*, June 7, 2010.

Lauren Kirchner   "Why Amazon Caved, and What It Means for the Rest of Us," *Columbia Journalism Review*, December 3, 2010.

Louis Klarevas "WikiLeaks, the Web, and the Need to Rethink the Espionage Act," *The New York Times*, December 9, 2010.

David Kushner "Inside WikiLeaks' Leak Factory," *Mother Jones*, April 6, 2010.

Los Angeles Times "WikiLeaks Wasn't Wrong," July 26, 2010.

Ewen MacAskill "WikiLeaks Website Pulled by Amazon After U.S. Political Pressure," *The Guardian*, December 2, 2010.

Rebecca MacKinnon "'Internet Freedom' in the Age of Assange," ForeignPolicy.com, February 17, 2011.

Alex Massie "Yes, Julian Assange Is a Journalist," *The Spectator*, November 2, 2010.

Elisa Massimino "WikiLeaks and Internet Freedom," HumanRightsFirst.org, December 9, 2010. www.humanrightsfirst.org.

Evgeny Morozov "WikiLeaks, Julian Assange, and the Dark Side of Internet Freedom," *Christian Science Monitor*, December 7, 2010.

The Nation "First, They Came for WikiLeaks. Then . . . ," December 27, 2010. www.thenation.com.

John Naughton "Live with the WikiLeakable World or Shut Down the Net. It's Your Choice," *The Guardian*, December 6, 2010.

Alex Newman   "WikiLeaks Leads to Calls for New
                   Infringements on Speech, Press," *The
                   New American*, December 30, 2010.

Rainey Reitman   "The Best of Cablegate: Instances
                   Where Public Discourse Benefited
                   from the Leaks," Electronic Freedom
                   Foundation, January 7, 2011. www
                   .eff.org.

David Sarno   "'Hactivists' Fight for Their Cause
                   Online—A Sabotage Campaign
                   Backing WikiLeaks Claims to Be
                   Defending Internet Freedom," *Time*,
                   December 11, 2010.

Raphael Satter   "Exposed: Uncensored WikiLeaks
                   Cables Posted to Web," Associated
                   Press, September 1, 2011.

Charlie Savage   "U.S. Weighs Prosecution of
                   WikiLeaks Founder, but Legal
                   Scholars Warn of Steep Hurdles," *The
                   New York Times*, December 1, 2010.

Alina Selyukh   "Witnesses Testify in Bradley
                   Manning WikiLeaks Case," Reuters,
                   December 17, 2011.

Jack Shafer   "Julian Assange's Great Luck—Why
                   His Arrest and Jailing in the United
                   Kingdom Is Good News for Him,"
                   Slate, December 7, 2010. www.slate
                   .com.

Mark Thompson   "Combat Video: The Pentagon
                   Springs a WikiLeak," *Time*, April 6,
                   2010. www.time.com.

Joby Warrick   "WikiLeaks Works to Expose
                    Government Secrets, but Web Site's
                    Sources Are a Mystery," *Washington
                    Post*, May 19, 2010.

Cintra Wilson   "WikiLeaks Is Everywhere," *Hartford
                    Advocate*, January 20, 2011.

Ann Woolner   "WikiLeaks Secret Records Dump
                    Stays in Legal Clear," *Bloomberg*, July
                    28, 2010.

Jillian York   "Net Freedom 'at Stake' on
                    WikiLeaks," Al Jazeera English,
                    December 8, 2010. http://english
                    .aljazeera.net.

Fareed Zakaria   "WikiLeaks Shows the Skills of U.S.
                    Diplomats," *Time*, December 2, 2010.
                    www.time.com.

Index

A

Abdullah (King), 68

Abrams, Norman, 73

Afghanistan War Logs. *See* War Logs

al-Qaeda, 71, 74

Alien and Sedition Acts, 89

Amazon.com, 9, 72

American Civil Liberties Union (ACLU), 8, 82, 89

Amnesty International human rights reporting award (2009), 17

Anonymous sources

    dropboxes for, 11–13, 16, 20, 56

    information to WikiLeaks, 7

    security for, 22

Anti-war activists, 65–66, 93, 95

Antiterrorism and Effective Death Penalty Act, 71–72

Assange, Julian

    arrest of, 9–10

    Espionage Act charges, 71

    harm from, 68–69

    harm minimization policy of, 46–47

    investigation of, 94–95

    justifying actions, 53

    as news source, 33–34

    opinions about, 10, 26

    organizational structure, 56–57

    profile of, 31

    prosecution issues over, 7–8, 75, 77–78, 92

    publisher status of, 61–62

    scientific journalism of, 48–49, 65–66

    shooting the messenger, 67

    transparency assurance, 64–69

    as WikiLeaks founder, 25, 29

    See also WikiLeaks.org

Aum Shinrikyo cult, 71

Australia, 65–68, 72–73

Australian Department of Defence, 68

Authoritarian governments, 19–20

B

Badger, Emily, 55–63

Baghdad, Collateral Murder video, 7

Bahrain, 68

Baquet, Dean, 39

Bay of Pigs invasion, 59

Bell, Emily, 56

Beneficial leaks, 87

Benkler, Yochai, 100

bin Laden, Osama, 41, 66

Black, Hugo, 44

Burns, John, 37

Bush, George W. (administration), 42, 73

C

Cablegate.WikiLeaks.org, 7, 72

Catholic Church attacks, 18

Center for Advanced Defense Studies, 74

Central Intelligence Agency (CIA), 39, 59, 87

G

H

I